"Charting the course of her own journey through sorrow and loss, Lianna Davis wrestles with the theological and practical questions that confront any parent who loses a child. If God could have prevented this, why did He allow it to happen? If we are sinners by nature, how can we be sure that an infant child is in heaven? How do you navigate the enigma of being a mother when you no longer have a child to mother? How can you move forward when your heart holds on to grief and does not want to be comforted?

Made for a Different Land is biblically faithful, theologically clear and rich in godly wisdom. May God use this moving, compelling and beautifully written book to bring comfort, strength and hope to all who read it."

Colin S. Smith, Senior Pastor, The Orchard Evangelical Free Church, President, Unlocking the Bible

"In the weeks, months, and years after a loss a mother needs more than anything to know that she's not alone, particularly because the depths of grief are so isolating. When we miscarried our two babies, I was comforted by the words of women who had walked the same painful road. Lianna Davis has compiled a book that walks alongside grieving mothers, giving them biblical hope and a familiar friend. From stories of fellow mourning mothers to her scriptural reflections on her life after loss, Davis takes the reader to God and his eternal purposes—showing all who read that even in the darkness they are never alone."

Courtney Reissig, author, *Glory in the Ordinary*

"*Made for a Different Land* is a beautiful picture of what it means to grieve with hope. Lifting high the name of Jesus and his finished work in the gospel, this book will be such a help and encouragement to grieving mothers and those wanting to understand such grief."

Kristen Wetherell and Sarah Walton, co-authors, *Hope When It Hurts*

MADE FOR A
DIFFERENT LAND

MADE FOR A DIFFERENT LAND

ETERNAL HOPE FOR BABY LOSS

LIANNA DAVIS

with

BRITTNIE BLACKBURN, STEPHANIE BLANKS,
LINDSEY DENNIS, ABIGAIL EADES, SAM MARTIN, ASHLEE
SCHMIDT, MEG WALKER, AND CALLI WILLIAMS

NEW BRAUNFELS, TEXAS

Dedicated to precious babies
gone ahead from among us—

Baby A
Baby Walker
Blair Reece
Chance Michael
Dasah
Jacob
Kinley
"The Martian"
Maxwell Spencer
Noelle
Odelle
Paige
Sarabeth Marie
Simeon
Sophie

CONTENTS

Instead, they were longing for
a better country—a heavenly one.
—Hebrews 11:16 NIV

FOREWORD

Lianna came into my life about three and a half years ago when I first read her writing at Hope Mommies. Hope Mommies is a 501(c)3 non-profit organization for women who have experienced miscarriage, stillbirth, and infant loss. Each time a new post of hers was published on the blog, I devoured it immediately. She was able to articulate feelings and thoughts I carried in my heart for the Lord, and for my own daughter in heaven, that I had not yet found words to express. I felt a deep connection to her soul.

Through the years, I have had the privilege of watching Lianna minister to countless grieving mothers as we partnered on the leadership team for Hope Mommies. Her posts and comments were always dripping with the truth of the gospel and reminded me and other moms that our greatest trouble as grieving mothers was not that we were separated from our children for a short time, but rather, that our sin had separated us from our Creator for time and eternity unless or until we accepted the gift of salvation.

In *Made for a Different Land*, Lianna shares the story of her loss so that she can relate truths that helped her most during her grief. From the delivery to the funeral, from the first days and weeks at home, to attending a child's birthday party after loss, and on to life in the years after—she writes about her eyes being lifted to Jesus and being led through grief by him.

Woven in between the chapters of her personal story are the words of other grievers being one month closer, one Christmas closer, one Easter closer, one year closer, and three years closer to glory. A prayer of hope, an open letter to a contributor's baby, and a reflection on finally being in glory are also interwoven. Lianna and the other contributors have shared what I feel are some of the most sacred moments of their grief in an effort to bring hope where there can be hopelessness.

Reading *Made for a Different Land* made me recall my own grief journey and all that the Lord has done in and through my pain over the past eight years. The words of Lianna and the other contributors remind me to keep my eyes fixed on heaven and my heart anchored to the cross, where God holds his people near with his great love. We walk such a broken earth as a result of the fall and this world tries to rob and destroy all people and relationships through sin and death. It brings me to my knees in gratitude that this destruction is not the end. Jesus came to mend the wreckage of the fall and to reconcile lost sinners to a holy God through his completed work on the cross. This truth enables me to grieve my daughter's death with hope for both the now and the "not yet." He alone is the author of all things, good and redemptive, and it is only through him that we have the hope of deep and rich joy amid the sufferings of this life.

I have often witnessed how suffering grief as deep and wide as the loss of a very loved and wanted baby makes engaging in life again and having joy seem utterly impossible. When my own daughter, Paige, was stillborn at twenty-two weeks and five days, I was not sure if I was ever going to be okay again. It was all too heavy—the weight of my empty arms, the ache in my heart, the places in my home where she would have been but was not. Nothing felt secure. Everything seemed as if it were sand that could slip through the fingers of my clenched fists. My words were few and my prayers were often: *Lord, I do not know how to go on. I need you. Help me.*

Even now as I sit here writing, I cannot find the right words to express the feeling of losing a child to death on this earth. Horrific. Devastating. Earth-shattering. All these words are true, but for me, none of them fully convey the gravity of it all. The sting of death seemed very real. Kissing my daughter's face for the last time before handing her off to the funeral home was agonizing. How could it be the last time that I would ever see my daughter's face or hold her body against mine? My soul was downcast. My heart was broken. The reality of my child's earthly body being placed into the grave desperately begged the question, "Do I believe that the gospel is really true?"

In the weeks and months following her heaven-going, there were days when I wanted nothing more than to pore over the Bible in search of answers to deliver comfort to my broken heart. Other days, I was so overcome with sorrow that I could not even reach for my Bible. It was on those days that I was fed the Word of God through friends, family, and books written by mothers who had gone through a similar experience to mine. I longed to feel that I was not alone. I wanted to be seen and understood. I yearned to know women who had been through this fire, and not only survived it, but were thriving in life here on earth and praising Jesus still. I wanted to feel alive again. I wanted joy again. I loved God, but I did not want to forget my daughter—and that desire took a deep hold. When my heart and mind did not know how to make sense of it all, reading books on grief and suffering helped me find the words needed to process my feelings and view them through the lens of the gospel.

Oh, how I would have loved a book such as this one! Like me, Lianna's journey on this earth took a turn she never dreamed of with the death of her precious baby. Yet, she continued to love Jesus with her whole heart. She trusted that his sovereign plans were to prosper his kingdom and she believed that he had not forgotten his people.

Her story gives me courage to press on in this life on the days that are hard. Her words remind me that it was out of his goodness, and loving kindness, that he called her daughter home after only knowing the safety of a mother's womb. And I rejoice in the hope of how many babies he has taken home in great kindness! I rejoice in them being "alive, full, and free" in him—as Lianna has put it. I praise him for the biblically-based hope that so many precious babies of families I have bonded with through Hope Mommies, church, and other friendships, have received ultimate healing in heaven—even though it hurts that healing did not happen this side of the veil. I praise him that as a believing mother I have been given such an eternal hope that I can resolvedly call myself a Hope Mom—an encouraging name coined by the Hope Mommies' founder and one that is widely used within our organization. Hope Mom is a title that I proudly proclaim because it is only through him that I have the ultimate hope of salvation, the hope of reunion with my daughter one day, and the hope of experiencing deep joy amid the sufferings of this life.

God has a plan and purpose for the lives of his people—even in the hurt, even in the waiting, even in the tension of the "not yet." I pray that God will use *Made for a Different Land* to encourage readers, whether or not they have personally experienced baby loss, with great hope and gospel truths. And specifically, I pray God will use this book in the lives of grieving mothers for what they perhaps cannot yet imagine: to help them live again and be testimonies to the gospel. Because the gospel is true! And one day there is a great restoration coming: those who belong to him will be raised from the dead and joined with him forever in a holy and perfect place where the hurts of this life will be only a distant memory.

—Jennifer Parks
Executive Director of Hope Mommies

INTRODUCTION

When my husband first wheeled me into the labor and delivery wing of the hospital in Waukegan, Illinois, on April 16 with mild, but close, contractions, I still knew my baby mostly as a mystery. She was the secret within me who was waiting and wanting to be told. And I—*yes, I*—was guaranteed to be in the audience at the secret's first telling. In labor, gowned and lying on the hospital bed, ready to resolve the mystery once and for all, the young nurse-in-training told me that the heartbeat was sometimes difficult to locate, especially when forty-two weeks along and while in labor. While searching my belly with the heartbeat monitor, she reached down to turn up the volume a couple of times. I turned my head to the other side of the bed and saw a reassuring look on my husband's face. He only saw alarm on mine.

A second nurse tried. She opened the door with a force that told me she had been working in the hospital for some time. She took only two swipes over me with the wand. As she left the room to find yet another medical professional, I told her I needed a doctor. She looked back briefly and only nodded. My husband and I did not say a word; I could scarcely look at him. No longer did I only find reassurance on his face.

Then, an ultrasound machine and doctor materialized more quickly than I knew was possible in a hospital. I had only known hospitals to be synonymous with waiting—waiting after a mild concussion as a teenager, waiting after slipping on ice as a newly-wed—but I learned that a hospital could be known for swiftness too. I looked at the ultrasound machine's screen with desperation, but I did not look too closely—anything to maintain some hope for a beating heart.

The doctor sat at the foot of the hospital bed while my husband of six years, Tyler, sat in a chair close to my pleading face. Both nurses stood fixed in their spots, their attention on the machine. From the time the doctor first appeared, his face looked too long, and his gray hair stood up in the wrong places, like he had been delivering babies for a week straight. He looked at us. His countenance and eyes now matched his appearance. They were clear in meaning even before his words escaped. Three failed attempts to locate the heartbeat meant that the failure was no longer of the medical staff to find a heartbeat. The failure was of a heartbeat to exist.

I was accustomed to listening to her heartbeat at each of my doctor appointments. It was the sound that removed some of the mystery during her growing months in the womb and assured me that all would be unveiled one day soon. I took the assurance home with me. And in the quietness of my own home, I had a wealth of happiness knowing that a person—*my* little person—was within me and growing. The heartbeat said she was, and her movement also said she was. That quiet home and my motherly anticipation had only existed so that it could, in time, be filled.

At prenatal appointments when I still thought my wait would soon be over, I gained assurance that she would come. I lay on the exam table in the doctor's office and gladly received—through a beating heart made audible—affirmation that my daughter was exactly who and how she should be in that moment.

Yet, in the hospital that April day, the same assurance of her life did not stop when there was no heartbeat to hear. What I mean is, my daughter was still exactly who and how she should be. Parents want to know their child or children will "be okay" while growing and living in what can be a harsh and sorrowful earth. No, there was no heartbeat. But in the silence of the hospital room, I first had the inclination that she was going to "be okay" because she knew God. Through knowing him first, she became exactly who and how she should be. The one who directs our human lives planned every day of my daughter's life. She was made for the minute when she was truly free—*heavenly* free.

My parental heart was bursting for her already. The quietness with which she left this earth became her fullness. At the same time, my anticipation emptied, and I was stopped. In the past, when I extended my anticipation toward her future, it was met with her own anticipation in the sound of that familiar, beating heart that was readying for life outside of the womb. I imagined the beat would turn into other rhythms of life that would fill my days: her cries, her needs, and my ability to soothe. Now, that had vanished.

In the days and months following her death, I found myself questioning if it all really happened; I felt I had no proof that my time with her was real. Anticipation continues to be a theme of my life because I still wait; there is still quietness in my life that I am waiting to see filled, a mystery unresolved.

God calls all Christians to wait with a different mystery—that of heaven. I have heavenly lungs and a heavenly heart beating within me, ready to be born there. I am ready for what is mysterious to become sight. I am ready to see him. Whatever that will mean, I know that it will be good. Childbirth is the mystery that seems closest to this heavenly one. I was ready to see my daughter. As someone who had yet to hold her own child in her arms, I simply knew that whatever that would mean, it would be good.

We learned that a child was within, and everything changed immediately. Somehow, we were already so very in love. The pregnancy evolved from pink lines to grainy pictures to precious kicks. We felt this child though we could not see her. We saw the evidence that she was growing, but we did not yet fully know her. In most cases, the mystery is fully and joyfully resolved, through the journey of a baby through her mother's body, a culmination of pain and work. And after hours of labor, it was resolved for us—though only in part because I still wait to *meet* someone I have *seen*.

I did not yet know that the new quietness beginning that day would grow into a hopeful, heavenly anticipation. I did not know that God would be my truest doctor when the earthly doctor had no more answers. I did not know that I would grow accustomed to visiting him, instead of my earthly doctor, to gain my assurances. I would visit him to listen to the heartbeat of heaven where I hoped that my girl was very much alive—with life most real. I did not know that I would learn to breathe deeply with those heavenly lungs and be sustained from the beating of a heavenly heart. I did not know because I had never grieved like this before.

My experience is one in a myriad of experiences of bereaved mothers whose babies have gone ahead from this earth far sooner than anticipated. I imagine that many readers opening this book have experienced baby loss, readers I am so very sorry to welcome under such circumstances. Welcome to you.

Other readers may know or be seeking to minister to those who have experienced baby loss. Still others may be reading to hear of hope evident through grief and suffering. Welcome to you as well.

The pages ahead are filled with chapters about receiving comfort from God, resolving feelings of being misunderstood and purposeless, grasping hope amidst the cyclical nature of grief, finding ways to rejoice with those who rejoice, loving for God's sake, discovering reasons for eternal hope, gaining peace through God's character, expressing gratitude for the shortest of earthly lives, grasping a biblical view of Christ that can sustain trust in God's goodness, and seeing reason to continue forward on this earth. Interwoven between these chapters are contributions from those who have known miscarriage, stillbirth, or infant loss—writing on critical days in early grief and what biblical truths were most helpful to them.

The contributors and I seek to become less private with our grief experiences in order to testify with emotionally rich and honest expressions as to how knowing God has breathed eternal hope into our hollowest days.

Together, we share the hope that all born-again mothers who have experienced baby loss will see their children again based upon the sacrifice of Jesus Christ. We collaborated on *Made for a Different Land* through Hope Mommies, a non-profit organization founded upon this belief. We trust that God is able to bring eternal purpose from baby loss, for he can be glorified and honored through the shortest of earthly lives. We are mothers who have been afforded a beautiful gift through our children's brief stays on this earth: greater hope in the Lord until he comes again. We also dearly desire that mothers who do not yet know this great hope would hear the truth of Scripture and be lifted toward Christ.

Praise him for his very precious promises.

AN OPEN LETTER TO NOELLE TRU DAVIS

STILLBORN TO TYLER AND LIANNA DAVIS

David J. Hesselgrave

My dearest Noelle,

Late yesterday afternoon your parents arrived at Vista Hospital in Waukegan, Illinois, with the joyous expectation of your soon arrival. However, between the parking lot and the delivery room, something went terribly wrong, and your heart stopped beating. Long before you were born at daybreak this morning, you had already departed to be forever with the Lord Jesus. Now as your great-grandpa, I write this letter to you. Perhaps I will not be able to write anything that you do not already know, but I will write anyway—for our sake if not for yours.

First, I want to assure you that, at a time when millions of unborns are unwanted and cast aside, you were not only wanted— your safe arrival would have been greeted with unspeakable joy. Awaiting you was a beautifully decorated bedroom, a crib with toys to entertain you during waking hours and quiet music to help you sleep, a playpen replete with snuggly stuffed animals, and your own private closet well-stocked with play suits and flouncy dresses. Oh yes, indeed, you would have been welcome—so very, very welcome!

Second, I want to confirm the fact that your parents are as wonderful as are to be found anywhere—and that goes for your grandparents as well. There are many confirmations of this, but I will cite just one. Already some weeks ago, your mommy and daddy planned for your months and years beyond babyhood. On the lower level of their home, away from the hustle and bustle of ordinary living, they set up a learning center and furnished it with a little desk, a good-sized white board, a variety of games, and a number of fascinating books. Given the state of homes and schools these days, it is most encouraging to realize that you, Noelle, would have had wonderful care, wholesome upbringing and wise instruction. And, best of all, from them you would have learned about the Lord Jesus and his rightful place in your life purpose and plans. Yours are the kind of parents that would have seen to that.

Third, I want to say that, even though you departed so soon and with no time to get acquainted and laugh or play or even cry with us, you will be sorely missed. I do not know, of course, but in the providence of God someone else just may sleep in your bedroom, sit where you might have sat at the dinner table, and learn at your desk. If so, he or she will be more than welcome you can be sure. Nevertheless, you will still have a large place in our hearts even if—and when—someone new comes into your home.

Now, before I finish, let me shift gears for a few paragraphs. In the main, I have been writing out of experience—things we know from seeing and hearing and touching and feeling. Before concluding, however, I want to write out of Christian truth—things we know by virtue of faith, not blind faith of course, but biblical faith. Just where you are in your "by faith not by sight" journey, I do not know. We members of your larger family are at different stages in that journey. Also, the subjects I will address below are complicated. However, I will not attempt to "unscrut the inscrutable" but just speak very simply about three reassuring truths that we learn from Scripture.

1) Though we do not know the whys of your passing, we do know that it was within the plan of God and that it will ultimately work out to your good, our good, and God's greater glory. We learn this from the faith and theology of Paul (e.g., Rom. 8:28). We also learn it from the experience and testimony of Job. So with Job, we say, "The LORD gave, and the LORD has taken away; blessed be the name of the LORD" (Job 1:21).

2) Though we understand comparatively little about the outworking of God's grace in little ones such as yourself, we do know that the death and resurrection of his Son are what effects your salvation and resurrection as well as our own. In fact, concerning little children Jesus said, "To such belongs the kingdom of God" (Mk. 10:14). To be sure, there are numerous and very profound differences as well as similarities between your circumstances and ours. The Bible says that we are all sinners both by nature and by choice. However, though we all are sinners by nature (otherwise you would not have died), you yourself never chose to sin. That is a profound difference because the rest of us are sinners by choice as well as by nature. Nevertheless—and this is the most profound truth of all—if we are saved, all of us without exception are saved by grace through faith (Eph. 2:8–9). That is true of you as well as the rest of us. So all of us together turn away from the sorrow of separation and praise God for "such a great salvation" (Heb. 2:3).

3) And, again, although there is a lot that we do not know about your present circumstances, and indeed, about heaven itself, we do know that the same Lord Jesus who died and rose again

is the one who prepared heaven for all of us who believe—you as well as us, us as well as you (Jn. 14:1–3). Noelle, I must tell you (though you perhaps already know), this world has always been—and certainly now is—a beautiful place but also ugly, a pleasurable place but also painful, a hopeful place but also very frightening. It may well be that in his goodness the Lord Jesus took you to be with himself in order to spare you from the ugliness, the pain, and the trauma of this world. We do not know. What we do know is that he took you to be with himself in his heaven and that you can no longer come to be with us. But we know more than that. We also know that the time will come when he will take us to be with himself, and when he does, we will be with you as well. So please remember, Noelle. When that day comes, we will be looking for you. You can count on it!

I must bring this letter to a close. But before I do, I want to thank you. You passed us by so quickly, but thank you for not passing us by completely. Why? Because in your passing you enriched our lives immensely. First, you enriched our lives by reminding us that things that are seen are temporal, but things that are not seen are eternal. Second, you enriched us by affording us yet one more incentive to live our lives in the light of eternity.

Our (great-grandma's and my) deepest love,
Great-grandpa Hesselgrave

Chapter 1

Giving Birth to Death

RECALLING JESUS' PAIN WHEN NOTHING SEEMED TO BE AS IT SHOULD HAVE BEEN

Moments after the silence of the ultrasound machine filled my hospital room—and not long before I met my daughter, in part, in this life—I sat with shouts of tears, knowing I could not succumb to grief. My mind immediately recalled the story of husband and wife youth leaders in our church who had endured the stillbirth of their child. From this recollection, I was acutely aware that my night was not over; not only did I receive the news that altered my life's trajectory, but I still had to give birth.

I was to give birth when I already knew that birth's promise would be hollow. The hopes of life with my girl had been voided. Like a blot of ink over the hopes written within me, a black, seeping liquid now filled each crevice of my page. It seemed that I could look down at my hand to see that it had suddenly stopped, illiterate; the pen no longer functioned but was flooding. The page encompassed the space where my heart should have been.

If anyone could have peered from the outside—as at that point I seemed to do, for I became not only a participant in my life, but also an observer from outside of myself—he or she would have seen no heart, no stain, only a dark space, a hole. So fully had my heart been covered by the seepage. I would not have known where to grab for my heart in the void; it had disappeared.

But there was no mystery to the disappearance; my heart knew where it wanted to be. It flew ahead to be with my girl. If my heart were all I had, I would have ceased to exist.

I voiced in the hospital room, which now held my parents as well as my husband, that I thought I would soon die too. My living body was connected to death—a house to death, a companion of death. And the one for whom I served as motherly companion was my dear, whom I longed to follow. So, that hospital room turned, in my mind's eye, into an elevator that would transport me through death to heaven. I did not hope for death as much as I thought it must be; I did not plan to cause it, but it seemed inevitable. An alternate route through the events ahead that could result in continued living did not seem to exist. I mentally prepared for that fragile moment when life blinks out and a new reality magnificently overcomes. Perhaps both mysteries, the earthly one and the heavenly one, would be solved in that day. I was readying myself for more than a delivery.

And yes, if a heart were all I had, maybe my body would have followed her. But thankfully, there was more to me than a heart. The Holy Spirit within me overcame—not to usher in death, but to grant me further life. In one of those strangely divine provisions of life, and despite my state, I remembered two points from my past with clarity, greatly aiding my continuing life.

First, God is sovereign. When my college systematic theology professor lectured on the sovereignty of God years earlier, I felt as though he spoke not to the class but directly to me.[1] At that time, he commented how divinely aided he felt in the delivery of that particular lecture. I sensed the same, and I remembered. I was taught that ahead of difficulty, I must do the work to settle within me, resolutely in my heart and mind, the truth that God is sovereign. *God is sovereign*, I repeated over and over as I prepared to deliver my daughter. Though my hands could no longer clutch pen and page of written dreams and fumbled in vain for a vanished heart, they now had something to grasp: *God is sovereign*.

The second provision was specific, though I do not remember who spoke it. I was a child at the time, and when I heard it, I remember not only looking above me to this speaker but also far beyond to the day when I could be married and have a baby. The teacher considered stillbirth with us before I had realized this possibility could exist. Volunteers with our youth group had experienced this same devastation and all of us students were shocked to hear the news. The teacher helped us process it. Among his thoughts for us, he helped us have compassion for what the couple must have experienced. He considered with us that the mother learns her baby is no longer with her, yet she still must deliver. A process that is supposed to bring joy and life through pain, instead brings loss and death. I remembered this teacher saying that he imagined it to be one of the most difficult experiences someone could be required to undertake. As a child, I stored that information within, even though I did not need it then and had no reason to believe I would.

At one of our doctor's appearances, he told us that many couples are permitted to return home and process their loss in preparation for giving birth. This was not a possibility for me. I was in labor. I remembered feeling mild labor pains on the way to the hospital, but *where did they go?* I did not feel them; they were subsumed by the pain of loss. Yet, they were increasing as my body prepared to deliver my girl.

Just as I did not know of the hospital's swiftness until I needed it, I also did not know the full capability I had in the Lord until I required it. I believed that God would carry me through the time he had ordained. From somewhere else within, as though I had been turned on in a new way, I labored and delivered my baby even though I felt as though my heart had flown away. It was as if I was looking down on a scene below me, unsure if I should rejoin myself.

With a power not my own, I was carried through labor and delivery. I did not dig to my core to retrieve with my hands the strength I needed to push through, but his hands came around me and carried me, for in every way he proved able. *God is sovereign.*

The details of those hours in labor, which alone would have readily qualified as the worst experience of my life had I not lost my daughter, were rendered inconsequential. The physical was nothing.

In thinking back on this experience, my thoughts turn to Jesus' death. In the cavernous mental space, representative of the extent of my knowledge of what Jesus endured on the cross, this thought brings a small parcel of understanding: Jesus' physical suffering was inconsequential to the non-physical suffering that he endured on the cross. Imagining Jesus on the cross renders concepts of physical pain—the crown of thorns, the stripes, the nails, and the suffocation. Being in my labor renders thoughts of otherworldly pain, a late epidural that made legs useless, and my temperature cold, breathing difficult, body shaking, the efforts sensationless. Delivering a lifeless girl made the process lengthier and more difficult because a two-person job became a one-person job. But nothing worse could come than what had already come in her death: the physical was nothing.

On a different plane of thought, the same is true of Jesus. His physical suffering on the cross could not compare to the non-physical suffering. The outward lashings and crown of thorns, the nails and the crucifixion, are only an ironic reminder: if we only understand that exorbitant physical pain, we have understood nothing. The bodily pain could not compare to the likes of death and loss. Losing a child brings thoughts of a lost earthly relationship, an unresolved mystery, and the loss of the assurance that it—the motherly experience and new life within—ever existed. His suffering of substance existed in the realm of souls, sin, and death versus life. His relationship with his Father, an infinite, eternal relationship in existence prior to all human knowledge and understanding, was lost in those moments. And he knew the torture—the voluntary torture—of hell at the hand of the one whose relationship he lost. Believers do not have a high priest who is unable to sympathize (Heb. 4:15). Though this parcel of understanding about Jesus absorbs virtually none of the hollow echo in my cavernous understanding of his death, it tells me that, by contrast, he must understand all of my loss.

What I failed to be able to do—give birth to a living baby— God succeeded in doing *spiritually*. Jesus Christ, through the pains of infinite labor and groaning—but more, through punishment and receiving of God's wrath—gave birth to a new and living hope stored up in heaven for his people. God brings many sons and daughters to glory.

My daughter was born, and there was no cry in the room but ours. Yet, there had already been the cry of song in the heavenly realms that one more soul—her soul—would belong to him for eternity. For a moment in that hospital room, I thought that maybe I would not want to hold her, but only because my heart was already with her in a different place. I changed my mind in an instant because there she was too. I met her in part. And I was immensely proud to be holding my girl. Like any new mom I felt the flood of her existence—she was it for me. No matter what else I would do with my life, it could only be an added bonus compared to mothering my child (and Lord willing, in the future, my children).

Her baby body was made to be held, and so, we did for the entire time she could be with us. Desiring to magnify the reality of her life and our precious time with her, we recollected two of the preparations we made for her. A few days before arriving at the hospital, I purchased lullabies in order to make her first nights pleasant-sounding. During my last shopping trip with my mom, and after many previous failures, we finally found her bringing-home outfit. With these thoughts filling my mind, I also knew I had been awake for over twenty-four hours, yet I could not sleep. Instead, I lay in a hospital bed with an arm surrounding my daughter next to me. We dressed her in the bringing-home outfit, and I played those lullabies. My time with her was excruciatingly limited. *How could I be asked to part with her baby body so quickly?* And yet, her body changed over those hours with death's mean decay. I knew that it was time to let her body go because, after all, she was not there anyway. She was not there; she was made for a different land.

In those last moments, arms surrounding a body that would never grow, I saw her for who she would have been on earth—a daughter, another best friend with whom to venture through life, her own unique, dear person. Yet, I also saw her for who she was in that moment, who she is even now: alive, complete, and beyond me on earth due to heavenly perspective. In one day, we held our baby for the first and last times. The last time came. We did not whisper our love; we proclaimed it. Her body was taken from our presence, as was her soul hours earlier.

When we were leaving the hospital, the nurse who had helped deliver my daughter brought flowers. During labor and delivery, I felt like I was near death, so I cannot take credit for the comment she made: she needed to reevaluate her life based on the strength she saw in me. When she said so, I remembered that those moments with my treasure-girl were real. Even though I could no longer hear her beating heart, I perceived God's heart—his purposes—beating through us both.

Later, we blogged online to let our friends and family know of Noelle's birth into the fullness of glory:

She was made for a different land.

On April 13, we went to the hospital for a routine post due date ultrasound for our daughter. We were blessed to see her squirming inside the womb, see her adorable face, and have perfect test results. On the evening of April 15, we went to the hospital for Lianna's headache. Though uncommon, headaches can be dangerous if linked with high blood pressure. Lianna's blood pressure was perfect. Our daughter was monitored for another routine non-stress test since we were at the hospital, and we had perfect results. On April 16, Lianna decided it was her relaxation day before her scheduled induction the next day. She remembers feeling her daughter move about happily, thinking, *She must like when I relax.* The same day, at about 4:45 p.m., Lianna went into early labor. At 5:45 p.m., she called the doctor and told him she had not felt movement for about an hour. However, after playing classical music, which her daughter loved responding to throughout the pregnancy, some good kicks were felt. About an hour and a half later, we went to the hospital. In the parking lot of the hospital, Lianna felt another movement.

Upon being checked in to the hospital, no heartbeat could be found for our precious daughter. She went to be with her God and know his perfect love on April 16. The two themes Lianna prayed for her daughter throughout the pregnancy were for her daughter to know the Lord deeply and for her daughter to be safe. God has faithfully answered both of these prayers. She now knows him more deeply and is more perfectly safe than Lianna imagined. During the pregnancy, Tyler would also pray for his daughter all the time. He remembers praying on multiple occasions for himself and Lianna to have strength to trust God if anything were to happen to their little girl. We know that God's heart is breaking for us. We also know that God has a sovereign purpose for this precious life and this loss. The Lord carried Lianna through labor and delivery, giving her strength that was not her own.

Noelle Tru Davis was born on April 17 at 6:52 a.m. weighing seven pounds, seven ounces, and measuring 20.5 inches long. We named her Noelle, which means "birth of God," because we wanted her to always remember God's love for her in sending his Son to earth. We named her Tru after her great-grandmother, Gertrude Hesselgrave, who is a beautiful example of a woman who has and is serving the Lord with her life. Noelle has features resembling both of us: Lianna's chin, nose, and eye shape with Tyler's feature placement, fingers, toes, fingernails, and toenails. We think that her lips look like both of our lips in different ways. Most of all, however, Noelle is absolutely beautiful. Noelle is our perfect treasure. We miss her immensely. We are leaning on the comfort of the Lord and are able to mourn with joy because of our assurance of eternity with him. Some passages that have been special comforts to us are Psalm 25 and 2 Samuel 12:15–23. Though we cannot bring her back again, we will go to her. We feel blessed to have known Noelle for the amount of time we did, and we miss her. She has brought tremendous joy into our lives. We and so many others showed her so much love while she was with us. We will love her forever. She was graciously spared the tragedies of life on this earth. She was made for a different land, and we look forward to the day when we will join her.

ONE MONTH CLOSER

Sam Martin

I am an over-sharer. I love to talk and write, process with other people, and I do not have many personal boundaries. This has led to no shortage of conflict with my much more private husband, Spencer, especially on our journey to grow our family. When we first started trying to conceive, I would talk to any and everyone about my cycles, when I was ovulating, etc. When we miscarried our first child, I wanted to share our loss publicly, but he was not quite ready, so I did not.

The one-month anniversary of our miscarriage was on a Sunday that also happened to be Valentine's Day. As I sat in church that morning, sobbing through worship, we decided to share our loss publicly and celebrate the deep love we felt for that tiny baby we never got to meet. It felt so right to acknowledge our first child on a day all about love.

A few months later, we were pregnant again. And when we found out our second baby, Max, had Down syndrome, I wanted to start shouting his worth to the world. However, Spencer was still reeling from the unexpected twist our life had taken, so I did not share immediately.

But, over-sharer that I am, as my due date approached, I started planning how we would introduce Max to the world after his birth. Knowing that he had Down syndrome and that we wanted to celebrate it, I decided I would post a photo on social media with this caption: "Fingers: 10/10. Toes: 10/10. Chromosomes: 47/46. Jackpot!"

But instead of that fun, funny, joyful post, we shared, "Spencer and I are privileged to share that our perfect son, Maxwell Spencer Martin, came into the world at 4:14 p.m. on December 27 and went home to be with Jesus at 4:44 p.m. While we are devastated by this loss, we rejoice in knowing that he is in the arms of our Savior. We appreciate your prayers as we walk this difficult road with full hearts and empty arms."

While there were so many choices and decisions that needed to be made in the fog following Max's birth and death, one choice was easy: we did not want a funeral, but we wanted a celebration of life! It seemed that so many people were only talking about how Max had died, while Spencer and I both found ourselves wanting to shout, "Yes, he died, but more importantly, he lived!" Our time of mourning would come too. But he had been here, and—of course, second to his being in heaven—that felt so vitally important to us. So instead of planning a funeral, we planned a celebration. Approximately 150 friends and family poured into my parents' house, ate barbecue, and basked in the beauty of Max's life. We had a slideshow playing on a TV, his hair clipping and footprints out, and a beautiful photo for people to sign as a guestbook that now hangs in our living room. At one point in the afternoon, a dear friend and pastor shared some words and prayed before we released balloons with notes to Max, prayers, and Bible verses. For days after, strangers found me on Facebook through friends-of-friends-of-friends to say they had found a balloon and were touched by our boy's story and life. Most of all on this day, we celebrated the God who gave and gives life. It was a beautiful day that will forever be a cherished memory.

Other than Max's celebration of life, however, everything else from that first month passed in a bit of a blur. I was recovering from a C-section and figuring out how to function in light of such a devastating and surprising loss. Then one day, I looked down at my phone and realized it had been one month. Somehow, the days went marching on, and I had survived them.

For a brief moment I felt proud and strong. I had made it one whole month: thirty-one days. I was still standing. And then an unexpected wave of grief hit—so much for pride in my own strength! I was supposed to be taking an adorable one-month picture of my little redhead, sharing his milestones, celebrating all that he was. But I was not, and it felt wrong, unfair. Seemingly every other mother got to celebrate this milestone day, but instead I was mourning.

I still chose to celebrate. On January 27, the one-month anniversary of Max's birth and death, I shared a beautiful photo of the balloon release from Max's celebration of life. I acknowledged the cruelty of the fact that I should have been posting a progress photo, but also stood on the truth that Max was whole and healthy in a way he never could have been here. I celebrated that he was with Jesus, even as I deeply mourned that he was not with me. I tagged the post #memoriesofMax—glorifying God for the gift of Max. And then I had another big, cathartic, ugly cry.

Each month after, during what should have been Max's first year of life on earth but was instead the first year of my life in the "afterMax," I shared a snapshot of our grief, our joy, our journey, our #memoriesofMax. If I could not share Max with the world in the way I wanted to, I could at least share the way he was changing it. I could share who I was becoming because I had been given the gift of being Max's mom. I could share the ways my marriage was growing deep roots in the midst of the most powerful storm. I could share the ways Max's Down syndrome had opened the eyes of so many friends and family to the beauty of that extra chromosome. These are only some of the ways God has worked in our lives through Max. Instead of approaching the twenty-seventh of each month with anxiety, grief, and despair, I could approach it with anticipation and thoughtfulness, deciding how best to share my boy that month.

That one-month anniversary was tricky. It was hard, and it was sad—a reminder of what "should" have been but never would be on this side of heaven. But it did not have to be a bad day. I grieved, mourned, and cried a lot. But at the same time, I honored, remembered, and celebrated that beautiful baby boy of mine. I allowed the joy of the Lord to be my strength in that time of great sorrow. It is a beautiful gift that grief and joy can coexist so mysteriously. I made a choice that day: I did not let grief steal my joy. Through the enabling of the Holy Spirit, I sat in the complicated intersection of grief and joy; I missed my child terribly, but also celebrated the blessing he was and will continue to be.

CHAPTER 2

Made for a Better Land

BIBLICAL REASONS FOR UNSHAKEABLE HOPE ABOUT MY BABY'S DESTINATION

In the days after returning home without my daughter, I sat in bed before the Bible for many hours, searching. Humanly speaking, my most natural belief would have been that my daughter somehow reached heaven. Yet, as Scripture teaches, those who can be assured of reaching heaven have personally accepted the gift of salvation from sin and God's holy and just wrath toward sin—securing glorious heaven instead of eternal damnation. This gift is received by faith in the Lord Jesus Christ, the perfect and holy Savior, who is fully God and fully man, incarnated in flesh, died as a substitute for sins not his own, was buried, and rose again from the grave victorious over sin and death (1 Cor. 15:1–7). My unborn baby daughter would not have had capacity to comprehend this message. So, I had questions about my daughter's eternal destination. I would need to either trust God in the unknown or see scriptural reason to believe that my daughter resided with him.

Looking at the vacant body of my new, precious child could stir no other desire in me than to believe that she was first held in his arms, if not in mine. And maybe I could find that to be true. But without Scripture, I did not want to trust it to be so. I could not start with my own reasoning because I knew I could twist the gospel by which I was saved into no gospel at all. If I reasoned that he ushers infants or the unborn into his presence at death solely because they deserve to be loved by God, then I could also judge that virtually all people are "good"—or, at least have such potential—and, by my definition, deserve to be loved by God in a way that frees them from his judgment.

By this, I could also believe away the existence of hell and eternal punishment based upon the merit or potential goodness of all of mankind. I could convert his sacrificial death—an act of incredible love for sinners who deserve damnation—into an act of obligation and/or an exemplary act. In the first, he would come to earth to appease man for the suffering he allowed man to endure. In the second, he would serve as an example of the way man could best live on earth until reaching heaven. Neither are the gospel presented in Scripture and so, are no gospel at all.

My own reasoning had potential to dwarf the holiness of God; I dearly needed Scripture to show me his ways. With caution for protecting the truth of the gospel in my soul, I turned to the Bible for resolution on the most dearly felt subject I had theologically questioned in my life: my only daughter's eternal salvation. I turned there with a mind open to whatever it might teach, because I also could not reason that God had no plan for the unique category of people to which my daughter belonged. I held to this: God and his Word are the standard of goodness and truth. I sought Scripture alone to inform my beliefs, especially at a time when I could be prone to trust my own reasoning.

The day before I began searching for these answers, I had given my daughter's baby body to a nurse, who helped to transfer her body to a funeral home, where her body was temporarily held in a casket before being finally placed in the ground at her graveside service. Her body was not yet in its final earthly resting place; neither was my mind assured of her heavenly resting place.

I started with what I knew. Scripture teaches the doctrine of original sin: all mankind born after Adam are born sinners by nature—with the exception of Jesus Christ—due to Adam's disobedience and fall (Eph. 2:3; Gen. 3).

Psalm 51:5 communicates the truth of universal sin: "Behold, I was brought forth in iniquity, and in sin did my mother conceive me." My daughter is no exception to this human state; those lost to miscarriage, stillbirth, and infant death are no exception. Yet, will they be in heaven? As many scholars commented over the course of my reading on this topic, it seems appropriate to pause and acknowledge that Scripture is not overt concerning the subject of the eternal destination of those lost in the womb and soon after birth. Therefore, my conclusions are held with hope and hands open to the God I trust.

In my search, 2 Samuel 12 made my Bible's pages—cradled in my palms—seem to grow weightier.

The story of 2 Samuel 12 begins with the failing of David, the king of God's chosen people, Israel. David pursued adultery with Bathsheba and arranged for her husband to be murdered as a cover-up after she became pregnant. As a consequence for David's sin, God vowed to take the life of David and Bathsheba's son. When David's son was born, the son became ill. David knew the consequence God had promised. He also knew that God alone determines the times of life and death. As a grieving father, David pleaded with God to save his child. He went without food. He sprawled himself on the ground. He put on his mourning clothes. Those around him worried for his wellbeing.

There, sitting in my own bed reading of David, I hardly moved. Although I was not fasting to plead with God, still, food was not my priority, and neither were my clothes. Those around me might have been concerned for my wellbeing, but I was not. I had only one subject on my mind: my child no longer with me. I understood David and felt that he would have understood me.

David had the emotional foresight to understand the reality of loss before it happened. He thought of what losing his child would mean—to spend the remainder of his days without his little one. He pleaded with God to allow his child to live. When his child did die, those around David were at first too concerned for David's wellbeing to tell him. David's friends talked amongst themselves about how to handle the news. Once David's child was gone, they feared that David would be thrust into a hopeless despair. Yet, when David learned of his son's death, he did not despair—he peeled himself off of the ground, washed himself, put on his clothes, and ate.

As I read David's response, I questioned with David's friends who were worried about him. *How? How was David able to return to his normal life, which consisted of moving, washing, dressing, and eating, so seemingly easily and so quickly?* I knew David loved his child. I read that he knew how to mourn. In the first act of this story, I felt comforted by these very observations. The opposites could not be true. I felt synonymous with David in his love for his child, and I felt comforted that he, inside and outside, embodied the familiar emotions and behaviors of grief while thoroughly pleading with God for this child's life.

But as David also knew, the chasm that is created when a parent loses his or her child cannot be quickly or easily filled—not filled at all except by otherworldly hope. Looking to David's Messiah and my Savior, Jesus, enabled me to avoid despair: "But we do not want you to be uninformed, brothers, about those who are asleep, that you may not grieve as others do who have no hope. For since we believe that Jesus died and rose again, even so, through Jesus, God will bring with him those who have fallen asleep. For this we declare to you by a word from the Lord, that we who are alive, who are left until the coming of the Lord, will not precede those who have fallen asleep" (1 Thess. 4:13–15). If David doubted or questioned the eternal destination of his son, would he have recovered as easily? Would a man so sincerely emotional, as evidenced in his first expressions of grief, now be cold? Even further, would David have recovered so quickly had he believed that he had precluded his son not only from earthly life but from eternal life?

I found in David's words the answer to my questions: "While the child was still alive, I fasted and wept, for I said, 'Who knows whether the LORD will be gracious to me, that the child may live?' But now he is dead. Why should I fast? Can I bring him back again? I shall go to him, but he will not return to me" (2 Sam. 12:22–23).

God's explicitly revealed consequence for David's sin was the death of David's son. There is a nuance here: the loss of the child was David's consequence, not the child's. In the story, David hoped that God would be gracious to him and allow the child to live.

If the child were destined to eternal damnation for not being in possession of saving faith, would not David have prayed for God to be gracious to him *and* the child, or even solely the child? If the only way for the child to reach heaven were through the child's life being spared so that he could later make a decision to forsake sin and follow the Lord in faith, would David not have prayed for God to keep the child alive for the sake of the child? If David were not positive that his son would reach heaven, would he not have made that his earnest prayer? Presumably, David made no argument for God to save his son on the basis of his son's wellbeing because David did not fear for his son's wellbeing. Instead, David said of his son, "I shall go to him" (2 Sam. 12:23). Upon reading of David's hope, my spirit recognized that I too do not grieve without hope. I say no less boldly than David, "I will go to her, my daughter." I will go to the heavenly home that houses the full person of my child.

While I knew that much of the grief process was still ahead for me, I assumed within myself David's mindset of hopeful truth and found the freedom to mourn or to get up and eat. I remembered with David that I knew the conclusion of my child's earthly story. She had started the beginning of a new heavenly life, a life everlastingly with God.

A mother with a child on earth washes used, sink-worthy dishes while her attention is fixed through a window to where her little one is walking and running through the backyard. That is what I imagined for me and my daughter while pregnant.

Yet, I will still always be that mother, but in a different sense.

While I sort through my everyday work—including the daily task of walking through earthly grief—I will peer outside the window of this world and "see" my child walking through heaven. What would have been my daughter's curly, blond locks illuminated by the sunset during after-dinner play in the backyard is, instead, the Son of God illuminating her eternal life. What more could I want for my daughter than for her to have him? There is no better gift; there is no better view of a child through any window than the view that I now have from mine. She was not made to play in my backyard. She was not made for this world at all.

My husband brought me food in bed during my scriptural search, listening to the thoughts that prompted my tears of happiness through tears of sorrow. We made new, sink-worthy dishes that would need to be washed, and I spoke as one caught between the sight of two worlds: the world where I lived in mourning and the world I could see ahead.

The pages of Scripture grew thick between my fingers with the beautifully weighty news of eternal hope for Noelle. Still, I questioned further: *How would God, the God who tells me that people are sinners from birth and the God who makes sure Scripture teaches that people can only be saved through receiving the gift of faith in Christ, also be the God of the man, David, who was comforted to believe that his child went to heaven?*

In considering that all people are sinners, there is a distinction to note in how one becomes a sinner—both by nature and by choice. Through the sin of the first man, Adam, the nature of all mankind was corrupted: "Sin came into the world through one man, and death through sin, and so death spread to all men because all sinned" (Rom. 5:12). All people are all born sinners because, in Adam, all sinned. All people would have done the same as Adam and Eve in the garden.

Then, all people are also sinners when they inevitably act based upon that sinful nature in rebellion against God: "All have sinned and fall short of the glory of God" (Rom. 3:23). If one condition—being a sinner by nature—already condemns people to death, what could be the significance of delineating between the two conditions, though both are separately true?

Perhaps, I thought, *this makes a difference to God.*

As time went on, I searched for others' answers to this question. Author and pastor John Piper brought this distinction about becoming a sinner to bear fruit in my mind.[1]

He looks to Romans 1. All people have been given general revelation, the evident proof that God exists because of all that he created. Through mankind's ability to reason, this proof makes all people accountable to God: "For his invisible attributes, namely, his eternal power and divine nature, have been clearly perceived, ever since the creation of the world, in the things that have been made. So they are without excuse" (Rom. 1:20). Even though the knowledge of God is evident through his creation, all people who are without Christ willfully suppress this truth in unrighteousness (Rom. 1:18). Those with a sin nature also become sinners in their decisions to suppress general revelation and be gods of their own lives.

When the sin nature from birth is exercised, guilt is incurred, and there is "no excuse" (Rom. 1:20). Bible teacher and author John MacArthur writes in *Safe in the Arms of God: Truth from Heaven About the Death of a Child*, "Scripture teaches that we are *saved* by grace, but we are *damned* by works."[2] Not all have access to discerning general revelation as proof of God's existence, for not all have minds that are developed to reason—not all have done the "work" of rebelling against God through suppression of the evidence of God's existence around them.

Theologians R. Albert Mohler Jr. and Daniel L. Akin agree, writing, "We will face the judgment seat of Christ and be judged, not on the basis of original sin, but *for our sins committed* during our own lifetimes."[3] These authors go on to highlight one particular biblical text of Israel's history in which babies are exempted from judgment precisely because they do not have "knowledge of good or evil" (Deut. 1:39)—indicating that these babies do not have enough understanding to deny their Creator God, and thus, are not held accountable.

My daughter's sin nature, corrupted in Adam, was never exercised because her unborn mind was not capable of comprehending the decision to sin or any proof for the existence of God. She never became a sinner by choice and is not in that category of those without excuse. Therefore, I have come to hope that my daughter has a type of excuse that God has indicated matters to him.

Having this excuse does not mean that she merits heaven. Her original, unexercised sin nature requires the atonement of Christ. At the conclusion of a summary of the development of the doctrine of infant salvation, twentieth-century theologian B. B. Warfield writes, "Infants too are lost members of a lost race, and only those savingly united to Christ are saved."[4] He continues by listing three conjectures that have arisen in the history of this doctrine: "(1) that some suggest only infants of God's people are saved, (2) that others suggest only infants of God's people along with some other infants God decides to set His love upon are saved, and finally (3) that still others suggest that all who die in infancy are saved."[5] To this last item in the list, Warfield concludes, "It is as legitimate and as logical an answer as any."[6]

The biblical hope of infant salvation is an opportunity to rejoice in the sovereign grace of God. Warfield writes, "It can only be through the almighty operation of the Holy Spirit who worketh when and where and how he pleaseth, through whose ineffable grace the Father gathers these little ones to the home he has prepared for them."[7] Nineteenth-century preacher Charles Spurgeon also found reason to rejoice in God's grace that he observed in the doctrine of salvation of infants.

Scripture saith but very little, and therefore where Scripture is confessedly scant, it is for no man to determine dogmatically. But I think I speak for the entire body, or certainly with exceedingly few exceptions, and those unknown to me, when I say, we hold that all infants [who die] are elect of God and are therefore saved, and we look to this as being the means by which Christ shall see some of the travail of His soul to a great degree, and *we do sometimes hope that thus the multitude of the saved shall be made to exceed the multitude of the lost.*[8]

Seemingly, God places those who have become sinners by nature and not by choice into a unique category of people—not expressing of personal faith on earth, but still his elect. At the proverbial heavenly gates, no other excuse will merit God's ears but the kind that Noelle has to "offer."

If this excuse merits his ears, I can have the hope that he will withhold his otherwise promised wrath (Rom. 1:18) and transform her through Christ's righteousness, by grace alone, to merit heaven.

With graciousness, Jesus speaks directly of his special consideration for babies. In Matthew 18:3, Jesus indicates that children, or those who have limited or underdeveloped understanding, have the kind of minds ready to receive him. Those who recognize that their natural perceptions of him are limited and underdeveloped, with no rights to him, are those who are actually prime for belief. All who believe become like figurative children before him.

Then, in Matthew 19:14–15, not only does he invite figurative babies to come near, but literal ones among the surrounding crowd. In Jesus' day, it was customary for parents to bring their babies to a spiritual leader for the bestowal of a blessing from one generation to the next.[9] When a request for one of these blessings comes before Jesus, his disciples think that Jesus, surely, is too busy. But, instead, Jesus welcomes it. In light of Romans 1:20, who would be more "like" little children than infants and those in the womb who literally have the limited understanding he endorses?

Special consideration unto salvation, by his grace alone, is given from God to those who humble themselves to be figuratively like children. And further, I believe that special consideration is given to those of whom the literal description applies—those who are taken to heaven from the womb or in infancy on earth.

With thoughts of God's welcome in mind, my husband and I planned our daughter's memorial service as those rejoicing in her eternal destination. We clung to the unshakeable hope of his grace for her eternity. We planned that a small group of immediate family members would gather at her grave, the place where her baby body would meet its final destination on this earth. Similarly, my mind reached its final, earthly theological destination about her heavenly reality. With hope in view, putting her body in the ground did not signify the end of what would have been her best days on earth, but the beginning of the best possible "days"—heavenly ones.

At the end of it all, she was made for him. There, in the place where he welcomes her, she knows him, and thus, fully partakes in the joys of heaven, the joys of her Savior. She and I share this greatest joy—to be living sacrifices unto him and sanctified altars to his saving name. For we both know he has sacrificed for us.

From the moment I learned that I lost my daughter, I was broken with a heart as lifeless as stone. His power alone could penetrate. Though my tears fell on my flesh, cementing the loss within me, he could make me moldable again. Though my heart had flown ahead to be with my daughter, he could create a new heart in me.

Even in its lifeless state, cemented and a runaway—he drew praise from me. Though I was already his, already saved, he "saved" me again in the knowledge of her salvation; through the hope of my own daughter to be in heavenly glory, I relived my own precious salvation through hers.

Thank you, Jesus.

Even now, Lord, make me an altar whose stone cannot help but to praise, for your blessed sacrifice is ours.

Amen

A broken ALTAR, Lord, thy servant rears,
Made of a heart and cemented with tears;
Whose parts are as thy hand did frame;
No workman's tool hath touch'd the same.
A HEART alone
Is such a stone,
As nothing but
Thy pow'r doth cut.
Wherefore each part
Of my hard heart
Meets in this frame
To praise thy name.
That if I chance to hold my peace,
These stones to praise thee may not cease.
Oh, let thy blessed SACRIFICE be mine,
And sanctify this ALTAR to be thine.
—George Herbert, *The Altar*

CHAPTER 3

What He Has Already Done

WHAT MORE COULD I ASK OF HIM
THAN HE HAS ALREADY DONE?

The day approached quickly. I had much to do before her graveside memorial service. Part of the privilege of being a parent is serving a child. What would have been a lifetime of sacrificial giving to and for my daughter needed, somehow, to be compressed into a few, short days. The preparations for her service were still concrete ways I could serve her. I determined to consider every detail possible.

Her fancy burial outfit and baby shoes; her tiny pink casket; the handmade service announcement cards for our immediate family; the white roses we selected to be in the shape of a heart—corresponding to our maternity photograph in which my and my husband's hands formed a heart in front of our daughter in the womb; the photographer and videographer who gave freely when we inquired about their services; the plan for the service to include songs, memorial letters, and Scripture readings; the hand-drawn, framed birth announcements for immediate family; the hand-crafted programs to be placed on each chair; the tent for the likely rain; the chairs to be placed in a semi-circle around her casket—she was part of our circle; and the white and pink linens to adorn the chairs were among the last concrete acts of my love directly for her.

I also made plans to help myself remember the service for years to come. I purchased an extra set of her burial clothes and shoes to keep as a memory. I ordered twenty-four white roses: half to adorn her casket as it was enveloped in its burial box and the other half to be dried in my home, a memory of this shared bouquet. Tyler and I did not want her body to seem alone until we join her in the grave. So, we planned to be buried on either side of her, with her between us at our heads—our names surrounding hers on the stone marker. And by the generosity of her great-grandparents, we could bury her where other family members had already been buried. Gifts of jewelry from my mother and father helped us complete the preparations. A tiny pearl bracelet was given to my daughter, as well as matching silver necklaces for us both. Tyler also gave me pearls to match her bracelet, which I wore to her service, and I made plans to wear them for every one of her future birthdays. I put all of myself into each detail because I had wished to do that for her every one of my days—put all of myself into raising her.

Now, even as I write about the few days leading up to her service, I remember what I was thinking. Through this entire time of preparation for her service, God did not feel present with me in any remarkable or unique way. When, prior to my daughter's death, I envisioned experiencing a traumatic time in life, I also imagined that I would unmistakably sense the presence of God. Perhaps I would feel his joy like when I first understood the truths of my salvation. Or, I would feel fulfillment from him like at the heights of ministry. Or, I would feel his power like during the times of most apparent spiritual warfare. But in grief, should I not feel his overwhelming comfort like never before?

Sitting on the floor while using a corner rounder on Noelle's service programs, I searched my heart extensively. Where was the sense of his presence I expected? Our plans and making of arrangements fit into the hours of our days perfectly. There was never too much to do for any day; the time passed smoothly. I placed a paper border around each service order. These programs had already been through our printer to contain details for the service—the readings, songs, and spoken letters. I embellished the bordering edges as if they were part of a little girl's scrapbook—white flowers and pearly decals. I traced each one with my fingers, lingering over and perfecting them—like God over me.

Working on the details of her memorial service, I saw that God was arranging the details of my days. Though I did not feel him as I imagined I would, my spirit remembered that God was with me. He was with me as he had always been with me. He was arranging the details of my life, and I could see it in the ways he brought together each one of our plans. There was God's personal presence.

His steady hand in my life also extended to some preparations of my inner spirit—unbeknownst to me—prior to loss and grief. Due to an illness that affected me most prominently prior to my pregnancy, I was still recovering from intense times of panic attacks; these attacks caused me to consider life and death anew. I also understood from the outset of my daughter's life that pregnancy is fragile. With death and the fragility of life being subjects of contemplation during pregnancy, I can look back to see that my blog posts during that time had a remarkable bearing upon my unknown future.

On August 18, I blogged a thought from Augustine, paraphrased by John Piper, while thinking of Noelle:

> Our love for Thee is far too small
> Who love another thing at all,
> Unless from Thy pure hand we take
> And love it for Thine own name's sake.[1]

Little did I know she would be in his heavenly hands so soon.

On September 17, I posted a quotation by C. S. Lewis: "God whispers to us in our pleasures, speaks in our conscience, but shouts in our pain: it is his megaphone to rouse a deaf world."[2] Little did I know that God was preparing me for a life-altering pain for his purposes.

On November 15, I blogged about death based on John Donne's words:

> Death, be not proud, though some have called thee
> Mighty and dreadful, for thou art not so;
> For those whom thou think'st thou dost overthrow
> Die not, poor Death, nor yet canst thou kill me.
> From rest and sleep, which but thy pictures be,
> Much pleasure; then from thee much more must flow,
> And soonest our best men with thee do go,
> Rest of their bones, and soul's delivery.
> Thou art slave to fate, chance, kings, and desperate men,
> And dost with poison, war, and sickness dwell,
> And poppy or charms can make us sleep as well
> And better than thy stroke; why swell'st thou then?
> One short sleep past, we wake eternally
> And death shall be no more; Death, thou shalt die.[3]

Little did I know my contemplations concerning panic attacks, that even death should not bring fear, were preparing me for the death of my little girl within.

On January 2, I posted a Jonathan Edwards quote about heaven:

If we seek for any thing in the dark by so low a faculty of discerning as the sense of feeling, or by the sense of seeing with a dim light, sometimes we cannot find it; though it be there, it seems to us to be impossible that it should be. But yet, when a clear light comes to shine into the place, and we discern by a better faculty, viz., of sight, or the same faculty in a clearer manner, the thing appears very plain to us. So, doubtless, many truths will hereafter appear plain, when we come to look on them by the bright light of heaven, that now are involved in mystery and darkness.[4]

Little did I know how greatly I would soon be benefitted by having remembered ahead of grief that the mysteries of this earth will easily diffuse into questionless-ness in heaven.

On February 26, I blogged:

I remember the different concerns I had at fifteen weeks— ones that I had to entrust to the Lord each day. I was already so attached to this baby person. Everything about pregnancy was so new. I don't think I had ever trusted him like that before—with something so dear to me, and so seemingly fragile and beyond my control. Today, I am grateful to him for such a smooth pregnancy—with no complications, with a healthy baby/me (and honestly hardly *any* discomfort, save fatigue!). His favor is overwhelming at times. I am waiting for my life to alter yet again—to earn for itself a new fragile set of concerns beyond my control that are presently impossible to understand. And I am anticipatory to live in a sublime day weeks from now, seeing my little girl and getting to know her. With all of those events ahead, I must trust him again and again. I know from his character that I can. And I really do—I trust him twenty weeks ago, twenty weeks ahead, and, by his grace, always.

Little did I know that the pattern I was building, of intimate reliance upon him concerning my daughter, I would soon need all the more.

On February 14, I blogged:

> The weeks have passed, and I grow and grow nearer to the inherent promise of pregnancy—seeing *her* and then seeing *her* start to grow. But the Lord knew my child long before my first broad smile on her account, before I cried fresh, wet joy at her first ultrasound image, and before I consumed her first kick. Think of the prophet Jeremiah of whom God spoke: "Before I formed you in the womb I knew you, and before you were born I consecrated you; I appointed you a prophet to the nations" (Jer. 1:5). Think of the psalmist David who writes to the Lord: "For you formed my inward parts; you knitted me together in my mother's womb" (Ps. 139:13). Surely he also deeply knows my little girl, the precious subject of my prayers (this promise is my joy, my confidence, my peace).

Little did I know how reassuring these verses would be when I learned that God ordained her life on earth to be briefer than anticipated.

April 16: She *truly* lived for the first time.

April 17: We held her dear body in our arms.

April 18: We blogged that she went to be with the Lord.

The precious start of a new life made me consider the end of it in death and remember that death is not an end at all. The great love I already knew for my child made me think about the

Creator who loved both of us first and was the source of our love. The fragility of being a mother reminded me that he gives and plans all of life.

Even from the first couple of months after discovering I was pregnant, I understood that I must love my daughter from his hand and for his sake. Surely these lessons and reminders, in specifically these days, could have only come from the school of God.

In the weight of grief, I searched myself for an overwhelming sense of his comfort within. Yet, as I looked back, I saw that he was with me then as he had been with me in the past. God saw me and ran his fingers over the lines of my days.

Having thankfulness for the provision of God's presence to arrange my days and thoughts both before and after my daughter's death was as relieving as it was counterintuitive. God had not provided the happy days I desired with my daughter, but he had provided much—especially when understood from the perspective of what I truly deserved. This is what coursed through my mind in those earliest days after loss, and it sustains me to this day. In his book of reflections on suffering, New Testament scholar D. A. Carson writes, "From the biblical perspective, it is because of the Lord's mercies that we are not consumed."[5] Because of God's good and holy hatred of all sin, every moment of my life on this earth can serve as a reminder that his just wrath has not overtaken me—someone who has chosen sin!

Every breath and every minute is pure grace, and that is not to mention the additional provisions I had been given, like the stamina to prepare for my daughter's service after giving birth.[6] Considering what I deserved of God's wrath, I knew my life to be replete with evidences of God's mercy. But seeing these kinds of provisions was only the small beginnings of considering what he had done for me!

God was still with me as he had always been with me; remembering that, I was refreshed in the scriptural promise of his presence (Matt. 28:20). He had told me he was with me, and he was. He had enabled me to receive an eternal salvation through which I will never be alone because of the Holy Spirit within (Eph. 1:13–14).

God has not been silent in my life. He has lingered in love over the human race. For he did not spare *his* Son (Rom. 8:32; Jn. 3:16). He has demonstrated his love in history: Christ's incarnation, life, death, resurrection, appearances, and petitions in the heavenly realms (Rom. 5:8; 1 Cor. 15:3–8). Surely, nothing more could be added to his completed work for me (Heb. 4:3).

What more could I ask of him than he had already done? I determined, *nothing.*

ONE CHRISTMAS CLOSER

Meg Walker

I made it through Thanksgiving—my first without Jacob—and was bracing myself for the holidays that would quickly follow. For some reason, the anxiety and dread about going through the Christmas season without my son, who should have been about ten months old, felt looming and overpowering. Maybe it was because after Christmas came New Year's, and after January came February—and February would be his first birthday. A birthday we would celebrate without him, because he had already met Jesus face to face. Regardless, it would be one holiday down with many more dreaded dates to follow. When I thought about those holidays, the heaviness seemed unbearable; I had a hard time imagining it. *I will deal with it when it comes,* I kept thinking, as my stomach sank deeper and deeper with every contemplation of the holidays with empty arms.

The Wednesday after Thanksgiving, November 30, my husband and I were sitting in the familiar ultrasound room where we had been for many of Jacob's ultrasounds, when he was still alive. During one of Jacob's ultrasounds when I was sixteen weeks pregnant, we received his diagnosis of acrania, a neural tube defect, which would lead to anencephaly. His skull, and therefore brain, would not fully develop. We spent one hour every three weeks in an ultrasound room, watching him kick and flip and grow, all within the safe confines of my womb. But after he was born, we had not returned—until that Wednesday, the day of the ultrasound for the sweet, new baby—Jacob's sibling—I had been carrying for ten weeks.

Again, in that ultrasound room, we heard words we never wanted to hear—previously, or at that moment. "I'm sorry," the nurse said, this time followed by, "But there is no heartbeat."

As I processed what she was saying, my whole body began to shake as tears fell down my cheeks. I noticed it the first time I glimpsed the baby on the screen. But still: *"No heartbeat."* The words were decidedly permanent.

Ten months after Jacob died and in the midst of the holiday season—how was I to survive this? A miscarriage so soon after infant loss. The thought was devastating.

My body held onto the baby as long as the doctors would allow, and as I sat in my living room two weeks later recovering from our loss, I remember thinking, *I do not even want a Christmas tree this year.*

The energy required to simply live felt too paralyzing in and of itself, never mind the energy to celebrate Christmas in my usual way. There were no presents for Jacob to go under the tree, no goodies for his stocking. There were no Christmas songs to sing for him, and again, our Christmas card was going to be empty. It would be just the two of us pictured—and no exciting pregnancy announcement like I had dreamed of.

I had no energy to bake cookies, and I barely had the spiritual awareness to even think about the season's meaning. Mary carried a son—the very Son of God—whose death was actually the reason that my babies were still alive—in heaven. Jesus, the anticipated Savior, rose from the grave and is exalted above every name and seated on the throne—but he came in humility as a baby, born to a young woman in a stable.

The year prior, when I was still pregnant with Jacob, Christmastime felt sacred as I remembered Mary, carrying a baby who was going to die. But now, with empty arms and an aching heart, twice in one year, and being expected (even if by no one more so than myself) to be joyful and celebrate "the most wonderful time of the year" felt cruel, painful.

And so, I did what I could do. I did the next thing. And on a whim, one weekend evening, my husband and I got a Christmas tree. It was not a perfect tree—it was short and a little stocky, and the tip was broken off. It felt fitting to me, in an odd way. Jacob was short, and chunky, and specially formed by God—not perfect in the world's eyes, but whole in God's. *This was Jacob's tree,* I thought, as I looked at it with twinkle lights.

All of the typical Christmas celebrations went on the back burner that season, but in our own special way, and in our own special timing, we celebrated as we could. Because I was in shock and our miscarriage was too fresh and painful, I could not begin to process it. I had to continue going forward just missing Jacob— who would have been born and with us—and let the pieces fall as they would. The most I could do was the littlest of things, like sitting by the tree in our living room with the lights on, resting.

One evening in the midst of all the tension and all the simply being, I remember feeling overwhelmed by how sad I was that Jacob was not there with us. Even though it had been ten months since we said goodbye, all of his things still sat in a corner of our room virtually untouched. And so, for the first time since the earliest days of my grief, I began going through them again. I opened up bags, and I cried. I squeezed his blankets and smelled the lingering newborn scent he had left on them. I allowed myself to remember.

I so wanted Jacob to be a part of our Christmas.

I sat and looked at his blankets, and while some of them were still safely tucked away inside a chest of his unwashed things, I decided that there were some items that I wanted to give away. In a burst of courage and bravery, and with permission from my husband, I gathered the extra hospital blankets, began cutting them, sewing the edges, and making gifts for our families to receive that Christmas. He was not there to make cute footprint reindeer paintings or new ornaments for their trees. But maybe, just maybe, Jacob could be part of the holiday regardless—a gift from his belongings that others would treasure.

I knew that giving gifts had been healing for me in the past, and the longer I worked on creating gifts made of Jacob's things, the more the sadness lifted, and the pride I felt as his mother began to beam through. A few days later, they were finished. With excitement, I showed the final product to my husband. And I cried—out of relief but also out of pain and longing. Again.

Christmas morning came, and the dread felt just as hard as I had imagined. There was joy though too. In the tension of the emotions, I was determined to bring Jacob into our Christmas morning. So, as we sat in our parents' homes and opened presents, I lovingly divvied up the gifts among our families. I was a little nervous; it was, after all, a generally joyful holiday and I did not want to bring the mood down, but I also needed to speak his name. I needed there to be acknowledgement that we loved him. My family needed it too. Evident by their tears as they opened their gifts and the quietness that came, slowly we each began saying things like, "We wish he was here too."

I gave my family permission to grieve and heal during Christmas by being willing to be Jacob's mom, to give gifts "from" him, to say his name, to celebrate—it was needed. It had been hard grief work, and it was still so painful, but it was worth it. They were thankful. I was thankful. God gave me grace to make space for my grief.

A day or two later, we prepared to leave town for work, and so down our decorations came. I sat once more drowning in tears as the last box was packed up—it no longer looked like Christmas.

It was over.

As if the past few days were a dream, everything came crashing down once again. I actually went through and experienced and survived Christmas without my baby. *Babies.* Another holiday, another moment, without them. Jacob officially did not celebrate Christmas with us. I was officially not pregnant anymore. Grief washed over me. Anticipating the holiday felt like one thing, yet living through it felt like another. But after it was over and the last box was packed up for storage, it was the reminder, again, that life had moved on. My babies were still not here with us.

A thrill of hope, the weary world rejoices. It was that line from a favorite Christmas hymn that I had shared on my Christmas card that year, and here I was again, living that line out as I grieved our miscarriage. As I wept and cried out to the Lord through my pain, he answered me, showing me his nearness and care. As I wept through songs at church, I found their rich words about

God's character to be a balm for my soul. As I gathered the few things in a box that were symbolic to me regarding the life of our baby—the shoes I had bought in faith, my pregnancy test, and a few pictures—I took heart in the fact that this baby was in heaven. As I began to journal my thoughts and emotions, share with mentors, and even tell some friends different aspects of my miscarriage that were hard, I experienced steps towards healing. I was so weary, but in Jesus I could rejoice.

That first Christmas after loss was painful, but it was possibly the most honest Christmas I ever had. Torn by grief and sorrow, again, the reminder that Mary carried Jesus—a son who was born to die so that my babies could live—felt even more powerful. The holidays—some of the hardest, most painful times in grief—did not have to be made up of traditions and picture-perfect moments. They could contain both joy and sorrow. That is what Jacob had taught me all along.

The King humbled himself to be born into a hurting and broken world, live a perfect life that I never could, and die a death that I deserve—all so that he could rise again, conquer death, pay my debts, and reign forever. Joy came down to sorrow and brought joy again. That is what Christmas is.

CHAPTER 4

God Could Have Saved My Baby Here

GOD'S SOVEREIGNTY—NOT A REASON FOR BITTERNESS, BUT FOR PEACE

To say that God is sovereign is to declare that God is God.
—A. W. Pink, *The Sovereignty of God*

My feet stepped outside to meet solid, chilly rain in a memorable transition from car to graveside while being sheltered beneath an umbrella from the sky's canopy of open tears. I became a mother with a buried child days after being a mother with a child in my womb. I sat near the closed, pink form; my daughter's casket rested on a nearby platform. But I felt far from it, far from her, as I joined my husband and family around a nearby circle of chairs.

One of my treasured keepsakes from Noelle's service is a photograph taken while sitting in my place near her casket. The service was nearly finished. We—my husband, parents, and grandparents—had already read our letters to Noelle; the chosen verses of Scripture and song had been proclaimed as we followed the program written to remember her that day, written to remember God's promises of heaven.

Nearing the end, one song remained. It was summoned from our lips, our hearts.

Praise God, from whom all blessings flow;
Praise him, all creatures here below;
Praise him, above, ye heav'nly host;
Praise Father, Son and Holy Ghost.
Amen.[1]

The photograph I treasure displays the moment after we finished that "Amen." It includes four faces—mine, my husband's, and my parents'—whose expressions, though filled with sorrow and longing, hold a decided peace. We all lost the baby we already loved. Yet, it was well with us. The source of our peace was and remains God's sovereignty. I clung to it from the time it entered my mind in the hospital to the day we buried her earthly body—and, by God's grace, I will cling to it in hope until he takes me home as well. His sovereignty I hold near.

After the service, my grandfather sent me a note that put into words what our faces expressed.

You will always remember her memorial service and that can be to remember the reasons for the hope that was just as evident as the sorrow and, really, more so. There are many good reasons for that hope—just count them. Many, many thanks to all—but mainly to you and Tyler—that the reasons for hope were so evident and even dominant. How solidly biblical and thoroughly Christian!

C. S. Lewis wrote, "Comfort is the one thing you cannot get by looking for it. If you look for truth, you may find comfort in the end: if you look for comfort you will not get either comfort or truth—only soft soap and wishful thinking to begin with and, in the end, despair."[2] I can imagine no other doctrine to which this quote better applies than God's sovereignty because it might not appear, at first, to comfort. Believing in his complete control over all of creation and thus, over my life, means that God could have saved my child from earthly death and me from the devastating distance I felt from her—and did not do so.

In the hospital room, minutes after seeing the flat ultrasound that changed our lives, we believed he could, and we asked that he would, bring her back. We knew from Scripture he could: "I know that you can do all things, and that no purpose of yours can be thwarted" (Job 42:2). Though he could have changed it all, he did not. He did not for reasons that are beyond us, for as the apostle Paul expresses concerning the principle of the mysteries of God's will: "Oh, the depth of the riches of the wisdom and knowledge of God! How unsearchable are his judgments and how inscrutable his ways!" (Rom. 11:33). Because of God's unique sovereignty, I know that he planned all of my daughter's days before one came to be: "Your eyes saw my unformed substance; in your book were written, every one of them, the days that were formed for me, when as yet there was none of them. How precious to me are your thoughts, O God!" (Ps. 139:16–17). Though her earthly life was no longer, nothing but goodness continued to originate from him: "God is light, and in him is no darkness at all" (1 Jn. 1:5). Moreover, even through our loss and grief, his good purposes would be completed, for this is his character: "'My counsel shall stand, and I will accomplish all my purpose'" (Isa. 46:10).

If God is sovereign over all of the workings of the universe, the earth, and my life—if he really could prevent all of the evil and suffering in the world, including the very loss of my child—then why did he not?

Jeremiah, the weeping Old Testament prophet who was young and seemingly ill-prepared for ministry, was familiar with questioning. He lived his ministry during the time when God's people reverted to spiritual depravity following the death of Josiah, who had been a godly king. As God's spokesman, Jeremiah warned the Israelites about the impending destruction of Jerusalem and the precious temple, only to ultimately witness these incomprehensible events come to pass because of persisting evil.

The book of Jeremiah is filled with the prophet's questioning lamentation and God's listening ears. During the unfolding lament and grief, however, Jeremiah fell into an even darker hole—as my college Old Testament professor, Charles Dyer, taught (I am paraphrasing), Jeremiah took his question mark, formed it into an arrow, and shot it toward the heart of God. Jeremiah said, "Why is my pain unceasing, my wound incurable, refusing to be healed? Will you be to me like a deceitful brook, like waters that fail?" (Jer. 15:18). *The Bible Knowledge Commentary* gives background for the analogy of "a deceptive brook, a spring that fails" that Jeremiah uses to express his anger toward God: "The disappointment of a dry wadi bed [valley] that only held water after a heavy rain was a depressing sight to those searching for water (cf. Job 6:15–20)."[3] Essentially, Jeremiah said this: "Why, God? Well, maybe you are the cause of this pain. Maybe you are the one who promises and does not deliver. You make my pain incurable. I thought that with you, life was to be overflowing. But no, you are the reason my life is dry—you have failed to do what you ought to have done."

Jeremiah felt hopeless and questioned God's character: "Perhaps you are that deceptive stream." How did God respond? "If you repent, I will restore you that you may serve me; if you utter worthy, not worthless, words, you will be my spokesman" (Jer. 15:19 NIV). In the early hours after my loss, recollecting

God's words to Jeremiah bolstered my spirit because of what God provided for him: a way of godly grief. God's clarifying reply was the very comfort he needed. God's compassion was unmistakable, and his expression of hope, intrinsic. Jeremiah thought that his pain was incurable, especially if God himself left him dry. And yet, God sovereignly promised that he could restore Jeremiah; he could make Jeremiah's grief honorable and worthy, and he could bring goodness from the burial grounds.

God is in control of all things—yes. He could have prevented my loss, and my daughter could be in my arms—yes. But, he did not. He did not prevent my loss and could have, and yet, he is still good.

Though the truth was veiled to my grieving heart for many months, making it difficult to remember: he is the standard and definition of goodness (Lk. 18:19)—the one in whom there is not a hint of darkness (1 Jn. 1:5). He could have prevented my loss, and he is good. Therefore, based upon God's character and through his great power, there will be greater good out of the loss of my daughter than if she had remained here. This truth is my favorite piece of comforting hope.

I think that some of this goodness I must wait to enjoy in glory, while some of it I can see here. Not long after my daughter's birth into glory, I was continuing my weeks-long process of organizing everything related to my pregnancy. I came across my records from our first few doctor appointments, including my little note about what kind of prenatal vitamin to take. This thought struck me: *I took those recommended vitamins and did everything else I knew about or could think of to take care of my girl. Yet, at the end of our forty-two weeks of loving her while pregnant, we had no girl to hold. No matter how diligent my care, I did not prevent my daughter's death.*

Looking at that note alone in my home, I wept and plunged into the depths of my God in prayer asking him, *Why?*—for the purpose of, again, being sweetly assured of his sovereignty. If my daughter had been taken from us for no reason or as a mistake, I do not know that I could bear it. No, she was taken from us by the sovereign hand of a kind God who calls the deaths of his people precious in his sight (Ps. 116:15).

As I continued to organize all of our Noelle memories, I came across the contact information for the pediatrician we had planned to use. Through another wave of sadness, I remembered again that while she would not need the pediatrician because she was sadly not here, she would also not need the pediatrician because she was joyously not here, *but with God.* She was somewhere better with no need for a pediatrician. In fact, my sovereign God made her directly and only for that better place. As Lewis indicated, hope and peace were my foundations for continuing in this life through the perhaps unlikely route of this lovely doctrine. This was the foundation of my restoration.

God's words to Jeremiah, to believe again that the sovereignty of God meant hope, were infused with purpose too: "If you repent, I will restore you *so you can serve me*" (Jer. 15:19).[4] No one has identified this purpose better for me than our pastor, Colin Smith, in a personal letter to me and my husband after our loss.

As years pass, I am increasingly convinced that the greatest service we offer to the Lord is to love Him still in times of loss and difficulty. The trials of life, as Peter says, prove that the faith of a believer is genuine; nothing other than Holy Spirit wrought faith would stand and endure in the sadness and loss that you have experienced. 1 Peter 1:6–7: "Now for a little while, if necessary, you have been grieved by various trials, so that the tested genuineness of your faith—more precious than gold that perishes though it is tested by fire—may be found to result in praise and glory and honor at the revelation of Jesus Christ."

Trusting in the goodness of God's reign was my very service to him during the first minutes, days, and weeks of empty arms—prayerfully, a witness to the world of the Lord's work.

I could rest with him the mysteries of his will that were outside of my jurisdiction to know—like the reasons behind the timing of my daughter's death. And I could have certain hope that he is able to bring forth what is good, even from the grave. I knew from his character that not a single moment of separation from my daughter would go to waste. For he has the power to form grief into the shape of his glory. His truth endeared me to a connection that I have with my daughter—the shared purpose of honoring him. I felt the worthy weight of it: though my expression of grief would not be without fault, grieving the death of my baby was a stewardship of Christian witness that I could do well.

Only this God of supreme, utter goodness and ultimate, meticulous power could unfailingly deliver hope for restoration and purpose alongside of, and out of the depths of, earthly sorrow. No wishful thinking could have been better than the assurance that God was in control. And nothing could have more made my heart sing than being useful to him in those earliest days of grief by believing that doctrine with expectant peace.

Praise God, from whom all blessings flow;
Praise him, all creatures here below;
Praise him, above, ye heav'nly host;
Praise Father, Son and Holy Ghost.
Amen.
—Thomas Ken, *Praise God From Whom All Blessings Flow*

CHAPTER 5

Jesus Put Death to Death

BELIEVING IN GOD'S SOVEREIGNTY IS NOT
CALLING DEATH AND LOSS GOOD

When God acts, he does not miss, stray from course, or partially bring to fruition. When he acts, the greatest mountains move, oceans turn to land, and darkness turns to stars and sun. When he goes forth in battle, I need not wonder if his war will be won. With God, I need no questions. His acts are definitive.

What higher mountain did he move for me, what deeper ocean did he clear, what vaster darkness did he light for me, and what greater war did he win than, first, sin and then death? I ached to recall these truths as a lifeless baby lay in my arms. A mountain was on my shoulders, the swimming waters were too vast for a person hardly floating, and darkness had taken hold of my little star. The war with death *seemed* to be over, by all appearances; she would have no more earthly life.

In 1 Corinthians 15:22, the apostle Paul writes, "In Adam all die." In Adam, my daughter died. Adam was God's representative in the garden—the first and, I trust due to God's character, the best possible representative of the human race. Yet, Adam sinned. Humans are not enough to save humans; I am unable to save others, and others me.

When I experienced death as an enemy, I knew in my soul that this was not how life was originally created to be. As loudly as I name death what it is, I say the same—even more loudly—about my sin. I shout that death is unnatural, against me, and had no part in God's Eden. But then, I would not have done better than Adam. My daughter would not have done better than Adam. We would have each chosen what was forbidden.

I am in the same situation as my daughter, even though she was brought to death sooner. I despise death, not because I am above it, but because I was born into it and am headed toward it. I am not righteous enough to rule over it. I cannot escape it. It is a mountain too tall to climb, an ocean whose waves I would never survive, and a darkness without light. No, death is not good. But I say it from the miry pit, not the self-righteous tower.

This rings true, even months after loss: death is not good.

I want to forget death, even now, but I cannot. When I look at my baby's picture—which never will be what it "should" have been on this earth—I see my dear one beneath death's hand. I remember that I am on a once-good, now-fallen planet. Though my daughter was perfect to me, in that she was all beauty to my eyes and brought only love to my heart, she belonged to an imperfect race.

No, humans are not enough to save humans. The story grows worse. I belong to a race of people born not only into the order of earthly death, but also headed toward eternal punishment for sins. When I write that death is not good, I write it helplessly. I write it without an ounce of accusation toward God, but rather, out of a mind knowingly responsible.

Now, when God saw such need, how could he have better demonstrated that he despises death—more than I do—than by finishing it forever himself? I am not left to wonder if his mission will succeed. It will, and it did. He did not slip through it; he demolished sin and death. Why? For he, the sinless one, *so loved the world* (Jn. 3:16). He made the mountain move from me to him. He wore the mountain—the incalculable weight—on his back and shouldered it until it was no more. Without drowning, he cleared the water, for he stood before its waves, like walls of evil, and he drank. The darkness never knew light like him—the kind that banishes every shadow. No corner of my life is left untouched.

He earned the victory. In the face of the baby resting in my arms, I saw death. I saw it on the baby body of my dear child. Is that not where death least seems to belong—on the body of a baby? I look at her picture often, and I choose not to show it to many people, in part because I do not think that many will be able to see her as I do. I see her for who she would have been without that dark cloak already covering her, and then, I see her for who she is now as someone who has experienced that he is the victor.

Again, I say it out of my need, out of my pit, "I despise death." I despise that death's unpredictability made life fall out of "order." Children are made to outlive their parents. My child was taken "too soon." Yet, death always feels too soon.

From that cry of "too soon," I have the triumphant "already" in Christ. Though earthly consequence for sin was hers and is mine in Adam, she and I have been given the "already" of eternal life in Christ. The wound of death is overpowered by the knowledge that death now ushers us both into God's presence. By Christ, death becomes new. For I exult in the second part of the equation: "For as in Adam all die, so *also in Christ shall all be made alive*" (1 Cor. 15:22).[1]

I dearly needed this newness. This truth, along with the truth of God's sovereignty, would slowly build within me in the coming months. Though I believed it as far as my daughter was concerned—*in Christ, Noelle has been made alive*—I had yet to believe it about myself again—*in Christ, Lianna has been made alive*. For my heart, though remade in recollections of his salvation, remained hidden to me since I was in that hospital room.

After we came home from the hospital and planned Noelle's service, I rearranged my bedroom. With little to plan or do for her, I at least kept doing. With help, I moved the bed to a different wall and went to the basement to find a dark burgundy comforter set that I had received one Christmas. I swapped the existing bedroom curtains for the set in the office, which happened to match the comforter. I found unused wooden picture frames, with a rich walnut stain, that I had once intended to collage on a wall.

I filled them with pictures of our new story: pregnancy and the graveside service. It had actually never looked better, that room. All of the out-of-place pieces that had yet to be used and which were not being saved for any particular reason were collected and put together like something finished.

My sister flew into town a few weeks later for a visit. I desired easy-to-be-around people like her—not people who would ask questions or seek to "do something" to help. Easy-to-be-around people were those with whom I could sit and not feel a need to thank—and not feel a need to put at ease about how they were approaching me in my grief. They did not need the reassurances that I felt understood by them or that they were doing helpful things for me. All of that required insight and emotion of my heart; I had none to give.

When my family was together and I wept suddenly—realizing that my sister's visit had been planned to meet Noelle for the first time—they were not surprised, they did not rush to my side, and they did not attempt to make me feel differently. They knew that my crying was the norm. Their eyes had compassion, but not desperation. They were not made uncomfortable. They did not want to teach me anything new but entrusted my grief to the Lord. It was good to be around people who knew me well, with whom I had already formed an ease of interaction.

Grieving felt hardly like the time for being taught, at least initially. Early grief was my time for pulling out of my past those truths that I had already learned—out of my "basement"—so that I could begin to assemble them together into something even more meaningful to me than before. It was the time for understanding that even though I had always believed in heaven, it now looked to my perceptions to be more real than this world. It was the time when, even though I already believed in God's control of the world, I now felt dependent upon him being sovereign over it for all my hopes. It was the time for realizing that even though I already believed that Christ conquered death, I now longed to see death die.

My sister's gardening skills came in handy during her visit. Our grass had yellow patches, and if we did not fix them soon, our homeowners association would be sending someone to fix them for us, at our cost. *Outside life was still moving forward? Had everyone not stopped like me?* My mom and sister repaired the patches while I sat and watched. I watched them dig the ground. That dirt did not know what it had coming to it. A neighbor lent them some yard tools because I owned none—such was the extent of my yard interests. They dug up the brown grass. Yet, inevitably some of the green had to go with it. They hauled it away.

I felt like the green grass that was removed with the dead. In Christ, my daughter was made eternally alive, like the new grass. Yet, while she was made alive, a part of my earthly life was cut away and tossed aside. My heart had been the hauled-away green so that something new—her life—could be planted.

Life is never going to be what it "should" have been, were all right with the world. As I write this book more than a year later with a new view in Lincoln Park, Chicago, I can say with renewed conviction that it is not what it "should" have been. Death is still an enemy, and one year later, I still resonate with that statement in the same way I did in the earliest days after losing Noelle.

Good *will* come. I will cling to praiseworthy truths I am learning. Beauty will come from this loss in a way only God could arrange, and he has glorious purpose through pain that I will one day see outweigh the sorrow of this world.

But, it must still be stated loudly that my life will never be what—according to the circumstances in which God originally created this world—it "should" have been. Pregnancy "should" never bring death. There is nothing normal about having a baby daughter who lives somewhere I have never been.[2] And there is nothing good about death in and of itself. I write these words from an acknowledgement of my human, in-Adam neediness, without bitterness—and, because of Christ, with a heart of worshipful hope. I write them, most of all, because I see in Scripture they are true.

My sister returned to her children and family after that weekend. Though my husband's employer graciously gave extra time off, he eventually returned to work. But I was not ready to return to much of anything. My daughter was living in glory, but I was not ready yet to remember that I lived. I placed my hands on the dresser of my bedroom and thought for a moment. *What if*

I do reject the Lord? What if I decide that all that I have learned in Scripture is merely one option—out of many valid options—for life? This lasted for a moment, but I did ask.

As I weakly attempted to stretch my soul away from the Lord, I found that it was made like elastic. When let go, it thrust into him more strongly than ever. *My heart has been tossed aside with sorrow. Death has become personal. My daughter lives where I have never been. Yet, if I reject him, I really have nothing. I cannot save myself.*

In Adam, all die. Yet, in Christ, all will be made alive. In Christ, death dies—it is finished. Out of the pits, I say it with a ring of praise to the one true God—death will be dead, no more does it sting. Christ is risen. He is risen indeed.

So, I live. I would remember it soon enough.

One Easter Closer

Ashlee Schmidt

Death shook my soul to its core.

It was the beginning of my fourteenth week of pregnancy when I went in for a routine appointment. Upon the first glimpse of my baby on the monitor, I knew that something was not right. My sweet baby was not as big as I had expected him to be, and he was completely still.

After a few moments of searching, our sonographer confirmed what I already knew to be true. His heart was not beating, and mine was aching. It seemed like my life was being siphoned out of me. I strained to breathe, and as I looked up at the monitor and stared at the stillness of my baby, I felt as though I was watching a nightmare unfold before my eyes. In that moment, death seemed to consume me.

When I left the doctor's office several hours later, I wept. All the way home I wept. And when I walked in the house and sat down on the couch next to my husband, we wept together. My body felt raw and numb as I thought of carrying the lifeless body of my baby inside me.

Six months after I found out that Simeon had gone to be with the Lord, I started feeling nauseated, and my stomach seemed to triple in size overnight. I was not surprised when the pregnancy test showed a positive result. I experienced such a mixture of excitement and anxiety. I was so grateful to once again be adding to our family, but the reality of loss was still so close to my heart that I was constantly aware of the possibility that I could miscarry again.

At my first doctor's appointment, I was knotted up with nerves. I had been praying all morning that God would anchor my trust in him, regardless of what lay ahead. As soon as our little one was detected I heard the technician say, "There is the baby, and there is baby's heartbeat." I could feel the tension leaving my body as I praised God through tears for this gift of life before me.

Several weeks later I went in for another ultrasound. This time, however, I instinctively held my breath as I saw the sonographer tense while she tried in vain to pick up the heartbeat. I felt a wave of dread wash over me as I realized that I was on this road again. The newest addition to our family would not grow up on earth. Here was another birthday we would never celebrate, another hand that I would never hold on this side of eternity. The weight of my pain was crushing and excruciating.

Unlike my first loss, I went into labor on my own around midnight. It was sudden and scary. The severity increased, and I headed to the hospital. Within minutes of arriving at the emergency room, I delivered our little girl. The nurse brought her to me so I could hold her. Weak and dizzy, I sat up and opened my hand to receive my daughter.

As I held Odelle in my hand, I was in awe. Her tiny frame was so perfect. As I beheld my daughter, and gazed in awe at God's exquisite handiwork, I was overcome with gratitude that he had seen fit to bring her into our lives for those few short months. I did not think I would ever be able to stop stroking her cheek or counting those beautiful fingers and toes. And I knew that even though I would not bring her home and watch her grow, I loved her completely. It was one of the most devastating, yet treasured, moments of my life.

Several weeks later, just a few days before my first Easter without my precious babies, I found myself battling the impulse to blame myself for their deaths. I sat down with my calendar in an attempt to figure out when our first loss had occurred based on the doctor's measured estimate of Simeon's gestational size. Part of me hoped that if I could figure out the date he had gone to be with the Lord, I could discover what I had done to cause his death. I felt as though I desperately needed something—anything—to blame.

As I calculated dates, I landed on Good Friday. In that moment, God, in his grace, redirected my heart. Instead of receiving confirmation of my fear that I might have been to blame for my son's death, I found comfort at the thought of Simeon being welcomed into the glorious presence of the risen King during Easter weekend—the celebration of the monumental moment in history when death was defeated. Death—that which has brought such acute anguish and despair upon mankind—has been quelled by God's own Son. Death has been defeated! It will not be the end of the story.

The death of my children was an excruciating heartache that altered the course of my life. There were times early on when it seemed as though I was being crushed and overcome by the weight of death. I wondered if I would ever escape its grim shadow. Joy often felt elusive, a betrayal of the precious babies who were no longer with me. At times, it seemed impossible to clear death's grief-filled cloud.

But through it all, I always hoped.

The first Easter after Odelle's death, I was reminded that I must continually reflect on Christ's death on the cross, and just as importantly, on what happened next. Christ arose, and upon his resurrection he laid death in its grave. As remarkable as it is that Christ died on my behalf, the story does not end there. Jesus rose again from the dead, and in doing so, vanquished death.

On that beautiful, marvelous day, death was swallowed up in victory (1 Cor. 15:54). Death was not the final answer for Christ, and I knew it would not be the final answer for me or my babies in glory.

Through his death and resurrection, Jesus obtained the "keys of death" (Rev. 1:18) with which he "abolished death and brought life and immortality to light" (2 Tim. 1:10). And while I still feel the effects of sin and death here on earth, I can endure because I know, from the depth of my soul, that death is not the end. Because I have placed my trust in the Lord, I can now stare death in the face and say, "O death, where is your victory? O death, where is your sting?" (1 Cor. 15:55).

Death lost its sting when Christ rose from the grave. Through his work on the cross, Christ overcame the power of death, and someday, because of his resurrection, I will be reunited with my beloved children.

As devastating as it feels to be separated from my children on this side of eternity, I rest in the hope that my babies were also given victory over death; they have received everlasting life and fullness of joy in the presence of my great God. Because he lives, my children have been removed from the brokenness of this world and have received everything that is lovely, joyful, and perfect. They are enjoying the pleasure and goodness of God's eternal presence.

When my heart aches to hold my precious babies who have gone home before me, I choose to look to the cross. My little ones are safe in the loving hands of God. Because of his great love for me, God sent his Son to be tortured, ridiculed, and killed in order to offer his forgiveness to me. Jesus' death on the cross made it possible for me to be redeemed. His death cancelled the debt I owe because of sin and satisfied the wrath of God. His death has given me life.

Because Christ rose again, I have also been raised with him, through faith, to new life on earth, and will one day be raised into eternal life in his presence. And the resurrection power that has been bestowed upon me cannot be undone. It is secure, unshakeable, imperishable.

So, when the sorrow that I carry feels too great to bear, I recall with confidence that death has been defeated. My death and my babies' deaths were overturned through the finished work of Christ. And when he returns, death will meet its final end.

On that first Easter after loss, I chose to fix my eyes on the cross and on the empty tomb that followed. And I will continue to keep my eyes on the cross for all my days to come. For it is there that my brokenness was mended, my greatest needs were met, and my hope was found, because death was swallowed up in victory!

> He will swallow up death forever; and the Lord God
> will wipe away tears from all faces.
> —Isaiah 25:8

The last enemy to be destroyed is death.
—1 Corinthians 15:26

He will wipe away every tear from their eyes and
death shall be no more, neither shall there be mourning,
nor crying, nor pain anymore,
for the former things have passed away.
—Revelation 21:4

CHAPTER 6

My Baby's Witness to Me

ORIENTING LIFE MUCH LESS AROUND EARTH AND MUCH MORE AROUND HEAVEN

It was weeks later, though not many. Tyler and I took our first ride to her finished gravestone. We drove as wounded people needing to be near to each other and near to the place where we could show some outward sign of our parental affection. I wore Noelle Tru's first and middle initials as earrings and sat with flowers in my hands. I looked out the window as we drove. The drive was long because it was our first time going back to Rockford, Illinois, an hour or so away. We were not yet familiar with the march of it—the speeds and the streets. Along the way, one of the songs we sang at Noelle's memorial service cycled through my mind: George Matheson's *O Love That Will Not Let Me Go*.

> O Love that wilt not let me go,
> I rest my weary soul in Thee;
> I give thee back the life I owe,
> That in thine ocean depths its flow
> May richer, fuller be.

We were on our way to visit the place where the bodies of those who had fallen asleep lay. As a twenty-six-year-old, I felt attuned to the destination and sensed a separation from those in the cars around me as they rushed on with their daily lives. No one else I encountered seemed to be going the same direction—at least that is what I visualized. For the first time, anyone ignoring the presence of death in their day-to-day lives seemed like the strange ones to me.

Out my little window, I took a photograph of myself as we drove. With photography as a new interest, I had started using self-portraits as a way to document my phases of grief. In this photograph, the landscape blurred, and I looked upward diligently. Were I not careful, my gaze would start to fall. My thoughts were prone to be unnecessarily deep and dark at a time like this. So, I set some self-limitation upon my natural initiative to feel her death within me. I did not want to be one with her in death without sensing myself one with Christ in the resurrection; at that point, were I to pursue the former it would have been to the exclusion of the latter. Having to choose, I simply reminded myself that he was risen.

> O light that foll'west all my way,
> I yield my flickering torch to Thee;
> My heart restores its borrowed ray,
> That in Thy sunshine's blaze its day
> May brighter, fairer be.

When my gaze did fall to the scene around me, I saw an old, collapsing house. *What was it doing there?* Though simple, small, and completely inconsequential, it did not belong in any upward-gazing eyes. It was the impostor. I looked around a bit more. *Is it possible that I live amongst impostors daily?* I do. I live amongst what tries to convince me—or by which I try to convince myself—that this present world is all there is. The dingy and that in disrepair. The broken and falling. These are my norms. I had grown so used to them that I had forgotten that I was not made for them.

But, death was not where I was going.

When I fall asleep, in Christ, I will find what is more real than my earth. I will find my heaven. He said he was preparing a place (Jn. 14:2–3). So, there is a place ahead that will be mine—and it has already been given to me, though it is waiting to be received. And it is already my heaven. I go toward it as though having already been given all the words of a glorious victory song.

> O Joy that seekest me through pain,
> I cannot close my heart to Thee;
> I trace the rainbow through to rain,
> And feel the promise is not vain,
> That morn shall tearless be.

Maybe I cannot keep this piercing clarity for each second of my life, but I can be changed. My baby is in heaven, the place where she is perfected, as I will be with a new body and full sight (1 Cor. 15:42–44). Perhaps therefore, she is no longer a baby, because after all, I am still a baby who will be transformed; I am a spiritual child growing up under my Father until I become like an adult, in some manner at least, like the firstborn Son.

I have the hope that my baby will be raised with a spiritual body able to walk, talk, run, laugh, think, and understand. I have the hope that she is with him. So, even now, I have the hope she can think and understand in a way that is holy, with knowledge of the holy, like I can yet only dream of.

Maybe I cannot keep these experiences, the piercing fragments of clarity, making them last into each second of my life, but I can be changed. In fact, this is my daughter's witness to me. I have someone real—a piece of myself—in heaven, a real piece in a real place. From there, she "shouts" to me that it is better, far better, than here. She tells me that earth is a prelude to heaven, not that heaven is an afterthought to earth. For as I glance upwards at my baby, I shift my eyes to the gleaming center of her world to see Christ standing in the middle of it all. I see him as though he is saying, "All authority in heaven and on earth has been given to me" (Matt. 28:18)—and he will give me my place.

I am changed. I have one more reason to believe that this earth is not my home.

My husband and I concluded our drive near the piece of land that holds our baby's body. We stepped out of the car and lay near her body on the ground. I found a single, white, nearly dried rose left behind from her service. I suppose I believe that God left it especially for me to discover, though I do not know for sure. I was not searching for a sign; I did not need it. But nothing could feel like a coincidence anymore. It was a reminder that the day we buried her would stay with me; I was always afraid of losing it. It was a reminder that my memories with her would stay with me, as he would enable. So, too, I would be reminded of that day when heaven felt more real to me than the ground beneath—the day I was able to thank my daughter within my heart for something new. She made me love Christ's heaven and heaven's Christ more.

My husband and I still plan to be buried on either side of our little girl in our own plots of ground. All around lay other family members, already asleep in Christ. All around—whether those we know or have not yet met—there is memory of many who have lived and gone from our present home as one day we will go. Surely, I *must* be able to remember that where I will go is more real than where I currently reside—if only because of those numerous gravestones.

As my parents wrote to me after Noelle's death, my future glory outweighs my present suffering: "In the following verse, the apostle Paul does not minimize the suffering of this life through which we now go, but uses it to help us understand the glory that Noelle is now enjoying: 'For I consider that the sufferings of this present time are not worth comparing with the glory that is to be revealed to us' (Rom. 8:18)."

I cannot bear this glory any more than Moses could have looked at the face of God and lived (Ex. 33:20). I lay by the tiny pieces of grass and ground that were cut away for a hole, for the casket, for the body that was previously a house to her most real self, her soul. I set the flowers on it. I swept my fingertips across my earrings that were her initials. The weight of eternal glory surely—though my grief weighed heavily upon me—must now be the heaviest to me. Even then it was.

I had been desperate for something else to be heavier, weightier, and stronger. The future that can call my present grief "light" and "momentary" must be (2 Cor. 4:17–18). The future that can make my elevator toward death in my hospital experience seem like a light experience must be weighty. It is heavy with the weight of those who have gone before. It is heavy with houses that do not need repair. It is heavy with bodies that resemble Christ's. It is heavy with hearts that are made useful to him. It is heavy with story upon story of God's work in refining to gold mere human strands of life. It is heavy with the glorious presence of Christ, for which I long even when I do not. It is heavy with the message that what I do here and now—how I grieve and respond to the Lord—matters dearly. It is heavy with the word forever—the concept beyond my comprehension—which requires that the pure goodness of his glory will keep going and I will look unendingly into it. It is heavy with my baby. It is heavy with my hopes. It is weighty—my eternal hope in Christ.

It is heavy, yet not at risk of collapse, because the one who holds it together is strong enough to bear each weight (Col. 1:17). I lean there fully. It is where I am meant to lean. For my *lifetime* is light and momentary. In it, I have been given a future residence that outweighs, a place where no impostors will inhibit my upward gaze.

Previously, I had become so familiar with my march toward death that it was somehow easy to ignore. But death need not be ignored; it also need not be my minute-by-minute focus—lest I delve needlessly dark. It is worthy of consideration, but it is also beyond my understanding. Above all, it is merely the door to a beautiful weight that I will be made capable of holding—a bright glory that I will be made capable of seeing.

The ground where bodies lay, where the work of my life will, in all imaginable likelihood, become forgotten, is the mere seed from which my living eternity comes. And how can I know it will come? Because his life is enough to raise plant from seed—what is mortal will be swallowed up by life (2 Cor. 5:4).

> O Cross that lightest up my head,
> I dare not ask to fly from Thee;
> I lay in dust life's glory dead,
> And from the ground there blossoms red
> Life that shall endless be.[1]

Knowing that heaven was the song of my baby—her witness to me—I remembered that it was my song.

I live. Love will not let me go.

CHAPTER 7

A Mother with No Child to Mother

GOD ALONE DETERMINES WHAT IS MEANINGFUL FOR ME TO DO WITH MY TIME

My daughter being born still came with a list of incongruous realities:

- Dear lungs that never filled
- Letting go of a child before she was born
- Death that dwells within the living
- Birth that will not bring life
- Waiting to meet a person I have seen face-to-face
- Simultaneously announcing a baby's birth and sleep
- A baby who sleeps before her parents
- Being a mother with no child to mother

I am a mother with no child to mother. I am a musician who cannot play music. I am a musician; I have the feelings and instincts of a musician. I played my instrument for a time, and it was precious to me. Then, when I was about to step onto stage and fulfill the purpose of the instincts, the excitement, and the practice—when I was to play the music on a grander scale and hear it myself in a new way—my music and my instrument were gone.

After being denied performance and thawing from the relative comfort of being in shock, there were many minutes and hours to fill. I had not merely anticipated one performance, but a lifetime of music. I was still a musician though I had no instrument or music—being a musician by nature does not disappear when the instrument goes away. Yet, I became weary of never doing what I felt made to do.

As a musician with no music, a mother with no child to mother, there were no other purposes I desired to fulfill.

Emptiness became the common thread I saw woven in these incompatible realities:

- Dear lungs that never filled signified an empty body.
- Letting go of my child before she was born meant empty arms.
- Death that dwelled within the living brought an emptied womb.
- An empty delivery meant a birth that did not bring life.
- I saw, face-to-face, my little person empty of life.
- Simultaneously announcing our daughter's birth and sleep was empty of an introduction.
- A baby who sleeps before her parents emptied my remaining life of my child.
- Being a mother with no child to mother meant days empty of motherly purpose.

Just as I thought my life might end in the delivery room, I thought that my life might end in the emptiness too. I imagined again that God might ordain for me to fly ahead. What else did I have on earth to do? I did not know. The delivery room once held the intensity of death. Though the feelings of intensity dwindled in the minutes, hours, and days after coming home, they dragged with the purposelessness that came from being hollowed. At some point I thought the dragging might come to a final halt.

Though each passing minute was less saturated with death than the delivery room, the feelings of purposelessness became more intense. While the delivery room days ended, and I lived, the seeming futility of my days encompassed my heart. I could not answer the question of what I was to do on earth, in this life. Heaven was more real to me than earth. Why would I not rather be there? Even the apostle Paul wrote it: "My desire is to depart and be with Christ, for that is far better" (Phil. 1:23b).

Purposelessness did not come because I did not love Christ and love Christ's heaven. I did. But I was beginning to love them to the exclusion of this life, and because of that, was partially loving them in the wrong way. Still, in the purposeless minutes, I remained open to the idea that I could be missing some needed perspective that would change my course of thinking. For being a mother felt second to one role only: belonging to God, not only in the life to come, but in this life too.

My resolution came quickly and suddenly: determining what was meaningful to do with my time in these moments was not up to me—it was a burden I was not created to carry! Recognizing this truth changed me in a moment. *God alone* could determine what was best for me to do with my time. Up until this point, I had not much considered Paul's next words: "But to remain in the flesh is more necessary on your account" (Phil. 1:24). God provided Paul continuing life, though he had desired to depart; so he knew it was significant to God for him to remain—for God's plans to accomplish his glory and for the good of fellow believers and those who would still come to believe.

Released from planning my own purpose, thoughts of soon seeing my life halt were lifted. But my days were not instantly different in other areas of felt-experience. They were filled trudging through the requirements of life, and mostly, sitting and remembering my girl. But on the basis of God's sovereignty, I determined that if sitting and remembering was all I was capable of doing, then I would deem it to be the most meaningful way for me to fill my time. How could I know what greater purpose he might have even in those times of tears no one saw? I could not know. So, I made the decision to trust him and consider whatever best I could give to be the exact fulfillment of my highest calling for that day of my life.

One day, I would need to move forward to other purposes in life that would in no way pertain to my daughter—new purposes that God might see important and fulfilling for me to have. I would return to existing roles too, but those were more easily reassumed. The new roles that I would never have done were my daughter still alive felt utterly alien.

I knew the day for new purposes would come, and yet, I still felt conflicted. I was still a musician who remembered beautiful music. It is music I sought to remember well, for my daughter was a masterpiece written by God. And like any good masterpiece, the effects are present long after the last note has been heard. I wanted to live the rest of my life simply moved by her music because I loved her.

Yet, I also had to ask myself: *If I dedicate my life to living for her, being moved by her, what could that actually do for her—what could that add to what she was already experiencing?*

In *The Great Divorce*, C. S. Lewis writes of a purely imagined, but heart-wrenching, scenario in which a mother lives for no other purpose than motherhood. She speaks with a "Bright Spirit who had apparently been her brother" about wanting to see her son, who is with God.[1]

The mother asked, "Well. When am I going to be allowed to see him [her son]?"

"There's no question of being allowed, Pam. As soon as it's possible for him to see you, of course he will. You need to be thickened up a bit."

"How?" said the Ghost. The monosyllable was hard and a little threatening.

"I'm afraid the first step is a hard one," said the Spirit. "But after that you'll go on like a house on fire. You will become solid enough for Michael to perceive you when you learn to want someone else besides Michael. I don't say 'more than Michael,' not as a beginning. That will come later. It's only the little germ of a desire for God that we need to start the process."

"Oh, you mean religion and all that sort of thing? This is hardly the moment . . . and from you, of all people. Well, never mind. I'll do whatever's necessary. What do you want me to do? Come on. The sooner I begin it, the sooner they'll let me see my boy. I'm quite ready."

"But, Pam, do think! Don't you see you are not beginning at all as long as you are in that state of mind? You're treating God only as a means to Michael. But the whole thickening treatment consists in learning to want God for His own sake."

"You wouldn't talk like that if you were a Mother."

"You mean, if I were only a mother. But there is no such thing as being only a mother. You exist as Michael's mother only because you first exist as God's creature. That relation is older and closer."[2]

I did not want to resemble this imagined mother, and I remembered some words my grandfather wrote to me after my daughter went ahead. When I first received them, I did not feel ready to read his final line, and I quickly set those words aside. But because of how I loved and respected my grandfather, and even trusted him with my heart, I was not tempted to push him away; I simply acknowledged the truth of the words as well as the difficulty of them, and then tucked them away for later.

But when that later date came, I could recall the words with gratitude for how my sights had been set on the truth early in grief—a plumb line for me, paving the way for full reception. And when I read them again, I could see that is exactly what he intended—a progression. So, these words were pivotal.

We may like to think that we are something, but the truth is that we are something we think. Not just what comes to mind, but what we determine to think—bringing thought(s) "into captivity." That is where truth, purity, beauty etc. come in. At first worldlings would think of Noelle only, seldom or never Jesus. As Christians we think of Noelle but also of the truth, beauty, etc. of "Noelle with Jesus," and that is not only okay, it is wonderful and healing. Gradually and increasingly, however, our thinking will center on Jesus first and Noelle second. That will bring the whole healing.

On earth, Jesus said, "Foxes have holes, and birds of the air have nests, but the Son of Man has nowhere to lay his head" (Matt.

8:20). Jesus indicated, poetically, that he did not come to build himself and his people a marvelous home on this earth where all that is good becomes fulfilled. But, he promised to build an eternal people of his very own, rescued out of this world (Matt. 16:18, 12:48–50).

Looking ahead to this eternity, I realized that what I was tempted to love in wanting to live my life as one moved by my daughter was actually not Noelle. It was the fulfilling role of being her mother, a cherished role toward her afforded only to me, but I had started to confuse the two. Dismissing other future work or purpose because it did not relate to her was not the best for her in any sense. It was not love *for her* because my purpose in mothering Noelle could never exceed my highest hope for her. And my highest hope had already been met: she already loved God most. The mission was accomplished—she was Jesus' very own, rescued out of this world.

As I prepared to move forward to new purposes, I loved my sweet song and remembered her music. I would always be a musician to her though I could no longer play. And I could see how her song had influenced me in the way I newly valued children, had new compassion for other mothers who had experienced pain, understood more thoroughly how my life could serve to meet another's needs, and experienced gratitude over simply being made a mom. I knew there was no more for me to do directly for her good on this earth. She was in the perfection of glory; I let go of playing that purpose.

Because I had unconfused the purpose from the person, I knew that I could embark upon new roles without diminishing the far greater loss of the two: her.

As I opened my hands and allowed them to receive other roles in life, a brand-new song slowly arose—loving Jesus, my first of kin and the "older and closer"[3] relation, the most was the best music of all. In my grief, I asked my grandfather to write devotionals for me when I hardly could determine what to eat, much less where to turn in my Bible. On my first Mother's Day, he wrote on Luke 11:27–28.[4]

It is Mother's Day, and it is special for various reasons. It is our mother who went through the pain of bringing us into the world and goes to most of the work connected to "bringing us up" in the world. Little wonder that Dr. Luke is the one who highlights what seems to be a rather offhanded remark by just another woman in the crowd—a remark that nevertheless elicits a "remarkable" response from the Lord Jesus. (She looked back and could see the baby Jesus at Mary's breast; but could not look forward and see Mary at Jesus' cross. The disciples could not picture that even when told.) In view of the fact that Jesus' human mother has been so revered and almost worshipped in some parts of the Church, Jesus' response is just as significant today—if not more so—than it was "in the days of his [and her] flesh." More blessed than being a mother—even *his* mother—are all those who hear and keep the word of God! *More blessed than Mary! That is amazing. It is a kind of "Mother's Day Card" to all believers—mothers, fathers, or childless.*

A MOTHER'S PRAYER

Abigail Eades

One August, we sat under the harsh, bright lights of an exam room and listened to the high-risk obstetrician list everything wrong with our baby girl growing inside of me. A week later we received confirmation of our girl's fatal diagnosis.

I was twenty weeks along with our second daughter, Sarabeth. And despite the doctor's predictions of pre-term labor, I would carry our darling girl to term. From the day we learned of her diagnosis to the day she was delivered, we had four and a half months to pray for her and beg God for a miracle. Miracles had been done before. Why should we not ask for one? God is able; he could heal our daughter!

We knew the God who stilled the storm on the sea and raised the dead to life. As I prayed for our daughter, many passages of Scripture came to mind that spoke of God's ability to heal and of the many miracles he performed. I felt encouraged by God's great power to ask him for this miracle: the healing of our daughter. I knew that he might not answer those prayers as I hoped, but I chose to hold on to hope that he might. The God of miracles was with me and loved our precious Sarabeth; I knew that the work he does is always perfect. This belief and hope settled in my heart as a deep peace, and I trusted that my belief in healing would be answered either in time or eternity. I rested in God's will.

The day of her birth, I lay on the narrow operating table, numbed from the spinal. And with my heart in my throat, I waited for the moment they would pull her out through the incision in my abdomen. We heard her weak little cry, but the look on my husband's face told me everything—she was not healed. She was alive but not able to live.

God did perform some miracles. The baby who was supposed to die in utero, who was supposed to come during pre-term labor, who was supposed to die within moments of her birth—she was born full-term, alive, and lived for seven days. We brought her home, and for one night she slept in her bassinet.

Twenty-four hours after we brought her home she stopped breathing for a terrifying few minutes. We called Emergency Medical Services and decided to transport her to the local children's hospital for assessment. My husband rode in the ambulance, and I followed. By the time I arrived, she was hooked up to many medical devices. She continued to have apnea episodes and was placed on a ventilator.

The next afternoon we made the heartbreaking decision to remove life support. It was clear that her little body was no longer able to keep going. She was tenderly placed in our arms, and in the quiet of that private hospital room, we wept as her breathing tube was removed. We cradled her between us and told her over and over how much we loved her and how she was going to be with Jesus. And then our sweet girl slipped peacefully from our arms into his waiting arms.

Originally, I thought the best way God could use our suffering for his glory was by doing a miraculous healing in our daughter's body; we could share with others his great power displayed in answer to our prayers. But I was wrong. God was in the process of accomplishing something greater and creating a more powerful testimony. He overcame in a more powerful way than earthly healing. He gave a perfect life for my daughter and grew deeper trust in me.

While only God knows the full purposes of our suffering, I do see he knew something I did not. He knew that my desperate dependence on him during this time of deep heartbreak would result in my heart learning to trust him like never before. And he knew that out of that deepening faith and trust, I would be able to share the greatness of my God despite my pain and suffering.

God's work in my heart through the loss of my baby and the hope I have of her life in heaven can serve as a stronger testimony to a hurting world in my life than had he healed her. I believe that sharing her life and legacy can be used by him to help other hurting hearts—in whatever way or ways he chooses.

I find great reassurance about the witness to the world of his greatness that can arise from heartbreak in John 13–17, which records the Last Supper Jesus had with his disciples before his trial and crucifixion. After washing their feet, he speaks to them of the coming trials and difficulties and what the Father has sent him to do. They have little capacity to understand the enormity of the task ahead of him or the significance of his sacrifice. But we know they are fearful because Jesus reassures them numerous times.

- "Peace I leave with you; my peace I give to you. Not as the world gives do I give to you. Let not your hearts be troubled, neither let them be afraid" (Jn. 14:27).
- "Truly, truly, I say to you, you will weep and lament, but the world will rejoice. You will be sorrowful, but your sorrow will turn into joy.... So also you have sorrow now, but I will see you again, and your hearts will rejoice, and no one will take your joy from you" (Jn. 16:20, 22).
- "I have said these things to you, that in me you may have peace. In the world you will have tribulation. But take heart; I have overcome the world" (Jn. 16:33).

Amidst troubles and heartache, Jesus offers the disciples peace, joy, and hope. This is similar to how he concludes his Word for us. In some of the final words in Scripture, Jesus gives us the promise of ultimate hope and peace. He *has* overcome.

> And I heard a loud voice from the throne saying, "Behold, the dwelling place of God is with man. He will dwell with them, and they will be his people, and God himself will be with them as their God. He will wipe away every tear from their eyes, and death shall be no more, neither shall there be mourning, nor crying, nor pain anymore, for the former things have passed away."
> —Revelation 21:3–4

PRAYER OF HOPE

Father,

Thank you for being my peace and joy in a world of such deep pain, longing, and suffering. Thank you for being my hope. Where would I be without you? When I faced the most heartbreaking pain—the loss of my precious, wanted, and much-loved baby—how could I go on except for you? How do I keep breathing, keep getting out of bed, keep putting one foot in front of the other, except by your strength? I am so weak and hurting. But your Word tells me that Christ has overcome the world. It certainly does not seem to be true when I do not have my baby in my arms. I confess that I sometimes doubt, and think, *Have you really overcome, Jesus? Where are you in all of this heartbreak? You are big and strong and mighty—why have you not healed more babies, allowing them to grow and thrive on this earth, and intervened to spare more lives?*

Some questions do not have answers except for you. Your Word tells me that you are peace, you are joy, you are hope, and you have overcome. You have spoken gently to my heart and taught me that overcoming does not look like healing every sickness and disease and preventing death here. It looks like deeper trust in the midst of painful loss. It looks like a solid foundation beneath my feet when the crashing waves threaten to sweep me away. It looks like greater love for you when the Enemy whispers lies that you do not care. It looks like finding thankfulness in the midst of loss. It looks like hope taking wings and soaring on the promise that you are with me, and one day there will be no more pain or tears. It looks like deep confidence in your promises when evil tempts me to doubt. It looks like being able to give testimony to your goodness even though I lost my baby.

Jesus, I pleaded with you for months to heal our Sarabeth. Trying to "bargain" with you, I promised you that if you did heal her I would spend the rest of my days proclaiming your greatness and goodness so that others could come to know and love you like I do. But you did not heal her like I wanted. Instead you opened my wounded heart to know and trust your tender heart more fully, and in doing so, you began a deep healing in me. You also healed my little girl completely by taking her to be with you, and you filled me with hope and joy and peace that she is safe in your arms. Ultimately, I know you were gracious to my daughter in sparing her from this world and taking her to yourself. Now, I trust in the ways you are working in my life to make me a witness to your greatness, whatever those ways may be.

Your peace is not like the world's peace; thank you for that! According to the world, there is no room for peace after such devastating loss. But I can still my troubled and fearful heart in your presence and receive peace that has no words to describe it.

Even now, you have given me such joy that no one can take away; thank you for that! I have shed many tears and been sorrowful to the very depth of my soul, but your joy finds me there and cheers my hurting heart.

And yes, in this world I have experienced heartbreaking tribulation. But your tender words tell me to take heart! There is hope. You have overcome the world. And I love that your promise is already complete—you have overcome the world!

And as I miss my little girl so much, as I miss holding her in my arms and cuddling her close in the night, as I long to look one more time into her deep blue eyes, I am exceedingly thankful for your promises in Revelation 21:3–4 that one day soon there will be no more pain or death or sorrow or crying. One day you will take these all away forever and ever. And God, you yourself will wipe these tears from my eyes. These tears that you see me cry and you collect in a bottle (Ps. 56:8)—you will once and forever wipe them away. You are making things new, and I am forever grateful.

Please, Lord, I pray for your joy and peace and hope for every mother reading these words who is heartbroken over loss. Please take each one tenderly into your arms and whisper your promises to her heart. Thank you, Father, for being faithful, trustworthy, and good. Thank you for your nearness, love, compassion, and comfort. Thank you for overcoming the world so that in you we can possess more than this world could ever give.

I love you, Lord.

Amen

Chapter 8

I Do Not Want to Feel Better

Moving forward is not leaving my baby behind

I decided to walk downstairs after a long morning in my newly decorated bedroom. I had changed it only because I needed something to be different to serve as proof that I still existed in a physical sense. I already knew I existed where I dwelled minute-by-minute—in my thoughts. Perhaps I would enjoy life around me, outside of my thoughts, again. But that prospect seemed distant, and I did not know how to get there any more than I knew how to birth the tears in my chest.

Despite the changes in my bedroom, the air up on our second story seemed dense. I felt my skin move through it—thick with thought and recollection because it was where I had sat most of the time since losing Noelle.

Out of my bedroom door and beneath a half wall in the hallway, I could see the stairway below me. The air became thinner—but I struggled to breathe it. I stepped down each stair, gasping.

I neared the main level but was not yet on it. It was the time for tears, but they would not come. How could I beckon them, and to whom would they listen? I heard their call, but how could I answer?

> O who will give me tears? Come all ye springs,
> Dwell in my head and eyes: come clouds, and rain:
> My grief hath need of all the wat'ry things,
> That nature hath produced. Let ev'ry vein
> Suck up a river to supply mine eyes,
> My weary weeping eyes too dry for me,
> Unless they get new conduits, new supplies
> To bear them out, and with my state agree.
> What are two shallow fords, two little sprouts
> Of a less world? The greater is but small,
> A narrow cupboard for my griefs and doubts,
> Which want provision in the midst of all.
> Verses, ye are too fine a thing, too wise
> For my rough sorrows: cease, be dumb and mute,
> Give up your feel and running to mine eyes,
> And keep your measures for some lover's lute,
> Whose grief allows him music and a rhyme:
> For mine excludes both measure, tune, and time.
> Alas, my God![1]

The hard stairs hurt my body, but not in the feet, knees, or legs. Those seemed like superficial components of me, conducting the stairs' impact directly to my heart. Every act of this world upon my body was felt first in my aching, swollen heart. At the same time, my mind insipidly processed repetitious, grief-dominated thoughts. From the heart the mouth speaks, and my heart was waterlogged with grief. My non-grief-related thoughts seldom survived—only the permeable, easy ones were retainable. Thus, my day-to-day conversations were shallow and terse.

My immobile heart cried to be lifted to new scenery; it could no longer endure the bedroom view. It called for help with its beating bell. Beat. Clang. But I refused to answer. I would have peeled my ears off if I could have, because far down within me, I had my reason for not answering the call. The pain was too precious to be removed. Stillbirth had robbed my house of treasure—the thief slashing my heart on escape. The pain was the proof that I once had a wealth even though no one had known her. The pain of that moment was proof that she was still treasured by me. So, the pain, the proof, was precious.

I paused on the stairs, leaning heavily against the wall. I lost those kissable lips, those round cheeks, and that protruding chin which resembled mine. I lost what would have been sunny laughter at the kitchen table when baby food covered her clothes and a telling, sour look covered her face. I remembered when days after her memorial service, I caught myself starting a familiar conversation with my husband, "I wonder if, when Noelle gets married, she wants to . . ." I caught myself. No more "when." I lost it all, and I did not want to lose anything else.

But my heart's clang resounded too loudly for my body. I could not hold any more thoughts in my bloated heart. Every movement and breath was felt in that sunken spot. I put one foot onto the main level of my home: *God, please comfort my heart.* I felt immediate regret for praying it. The only alternative to pain that I could envision was less proof of my heartfelt dedication. If comfort meant losing more of her, I did not want any.

My body pulled upward, and in a moment, I envisioned myself lying in my bed still—but now sinking. I wanted to be where I saw myself. But, at the same time, I could do it no longer. Through my sopping, my flood, the weight, the fragile, cracking, peeling air, God heard the call.

He received me and all my tears (Ps. 56:8). He helped me to understand that moving forward is not leaving her behind but moving ever-closer to her.

When I asked God to comfort my heart and bear the pain for me, I did not leave her while I moved forward because she was not anywhere in my past. She went ahead. How could I leave someone behind who was not behind me? I looked down to see that my feet were on the main level of my home, and the air's lightness now suited me. Tears were drenching my face. They suited me too.

I welcomed his comfort—the comfort that absorbed the flood created by my motherly love. When he did absorb what was sopping, when I could put two feet on the main level again, my expression of love had not been limited or devalued. Rather, his comfort proved limitless and invaluable. His tenderness added mobility where I stalled; when I was motionless, he brought me to new scenery.

Remembering that he cared for me personally did not come naturally to me after my loss, but I did not doubt his goodness. I did not doubt the essential truth that he cares. Yet, at that second-story half wall looking down the staircase before the new first-floor scenery, I told God that I was having difficulty remembering what I believed: that he was good. I was having trouble remembering that he was good *to me*. He did not answer my prayer to bring my girl back, to restore her beating heart. I had believed he could. But he did not.

So, it did not come naturally to remember that he might want to answer other prayers affirmatively, or that he would still want to hear my prayers at all. It also did not come naturally to feel like being answered affirmatively in any other area would matter much now. That was how I felt.

When I did not have the answers for myself, I prayed out of need more than out of knowledge. I prayed hoping that he had not changed, that he would still be the God I knew him to be before the loss he did not prevent.

I found that he was, and he cared—answering all my prayers as if by saying, "Come near, I am your perfect Comforter" (2 Cor. 1:3–4).

So, come all you springs of tears.

CHAPTER 9

The Freedom of Humble Grief

FILLED WITH JOY THAT SO MANY OTHERS HAVE NOT HAD TO ENDURE LOSS

I looked at the digital square on my phone calendar. A nephew's birthday party was that day in a few hours. I did not look long. I determined that I would try what I could. I could not move forward in life without trying. I knew that much now. I thought no more about it.

My husband and I pulled into the parking lot of the children's rental party room full of food, games, and bounce houses. We took off our shoes in the doorway. I had not worn shoes that were slip-on, and I took my time untying. I had also worn my hair in a different style that day: curly. My brother-in-law complimented my hair for, perhaps, the first time ever. That was sweet. It had not been long. All of their eyes still held compassion when they saw us—yet, most of all, when they saw me.

In the past, this nephew's party was held at their family home with fewer, closer people. Not this time. There were children, many children. I made my way to a section of benches and chairs. It was where the adults sat who had children old enough to navigate the bounce house themselves or who had babies still in car seats sleeping. It was where grandparents, whose children guided their own children; or the aunts and uncles, who did not yet have their own children; or the mothers, whose husbands did the rounds with their little one sat to watch. My husband and I sat on the benches together, belonging to none of those groups.

My husband was pulled off to play with one of our nephews.

I sat by a woman who attended the church in which my husband and I both grew up, where family still attended. I knew her by face, if not by name. Her eyes held compassion. She asked general questions of me, as I did of her. She was careful in the ones she asked. This was also sweet. I asked her if she had a job outside the home or was working exclusively inside the home. She answered. She asked me, carefully, what I was doing. I think she wondered if she had made a mistake. She had not, but I saw the compassion again. I answered: I had returned to work, starting a photography business.

I hung on her compassion and rested on that look in her eyes. If I try, I still remember every compassionate look that I received and every tear I saw being cried or was told of that was cried for Noelle. I applied each one to my account of love for Noelle, an account that I loved to see overflow.

Words were finished, sitting together on that bench, so she and I were comfortable in silence. I looked around. There were so many children, and each one appeared to be the apple of his or her parents' eyes—the laughing children, the crying ones, the whining ones, the elated ones, the independent ones, the outgoing ones, and the ones sitting in the corners watching other kids. I had one too.

I saw all of the children from a shared Sunday school class interact, and then, my nephews and niece interact. They knew each other. I had one that would have known her cousins too.

She "should" be here.

I cried. We left early. Most people seemed to understand—displaying compassionate expressions. And those who did not understand, I think, at least acknowledged that they could not, which was enough.

My husband walked out with me and started the car while I was trying not to trip over my non-slip-on shoes that I had made slip-on in my exit. He told me by his whole demeanor without saying a word that I had done everything well. There was nothing I had to be ashamed of. I tried. I did not fail. Next time, the next party, would be more possible because of that day. I would learn to better understand the grief. I would grow up into it. The grief seemed like a bounce house—a much tamer activity the older I would become in it.

In a perfect world, my daughter would have been there. But I have not yet been taken to that perfect world in which every tear is cleared. So that grief, the kind that reacts to what would not be happening in a perfect world, is good grief. It is not grief I sought to overcome as though sin, but the kind I claimed as true and honest.

Those at that little party with the compassionate eyes I remember —they, though celebrating, set that cheerful attitude aside for a moment to think of us and our loss. My grief became theirs, and their eyes showed it. And in deeper ways, that is true of closer friends and family members who adopted my grief, not only into those times I saw them, but into their lives. In that act, the verse "mourn with those who mourn" (Rom. 12:15b NIV) was fulfilled.

Someone who was not in a mourning state adopted my mourning so that, as each individual knew how, my grief also became theirs.

But I saw that it was no different for my portion of the verse: "rejoice with those who rejoice" (Rom. 12:15a). In my mourning state, I could adopt someone else's joy so that, as I knew how, it could become mine. In it, I could become overwhelmingly glad that others do not share in experiencing baby loss and do hold their living babies in their arms—that was, in fact, why I started my photography business. I wanted to gain joy through photographing newborns. I know, and perhaps, cherish in a different way because of my loss—how treasured is the joy of children. I know what it is to have and to not have. So, who is possibly a better fit to overflow with joy for someone else who does have children?

Charles Spurgeon describes this attitude—meekness—with words directly to the grieving heart: "Sometimes, when I am ill, someone comes in and says, 'I have been to see somebody who is worse than you are.' I never get any comfort out of such a remark, and my usual answer is, 'You have made me feel worse than I was before by telling me that there is somebody worse even than I am.' . . . The meek spirited man is glad to know that other people are happy, and their happiness is his happiness."[1]

One phrase I held dear to my heart was this: no one else has my Noelle. No one in that room had the one I wanted—*my* daughter. Through tears and sorrow, I still only wanted God's story for my life. And I knew that I had much. I had a sure hope for my daughter. I had the safety of my daughter. I had the best caregiver, God himself, for my daughter. I have a baby who, perhaps, is no longer a baby (1 Cor. 13:12), taken up to experience the glory of heaven. I have a child who is wiser than I am. I have a child who loves God most. I have a good God who loves and comforts me. I have the hope of eternity with him. I have the assurance through this storm that his eternity is more real than this earth. I have the opportunity to bring his name glory by how I continue to trust him and love him still. And in this very moment—each moment—I have him. I still have him. And I was not made to do this on my own. I can only do this *because of* what he has promised: "an inheritance that can never perish, spoil or fade. This inheritance is kept in heaven for you" (1 Pet. 1:4 NIV).[2]

The woman sitting next to me on that bench had babies. They were cute, and she had a kind husband too. I was glad for her. I "should" have had my own baby. But so should she. And she did. Praise God. She looked at me with compassion. Through forming tears before I left, I smiled toward her my broadest smile. Her joy became mine too such that a portion of my exiting tears were glad ones.

AN OPEN LETTER TO BLAIR REECE WILLIAMS

Calli Williams

Sweet girl,

There is not one day that goes by when I do not catch myself pondering what life with you earth-side would have looked like.

I held you in my womb while your heart was beating for twenty glorious weeks and three beautiful days. In my womb, I also held your shell after you had been in glory for four days. The four days leading up to delivering you were excruciating for my heart. The day my body fought to cling to you while a team of doctors and nurses intervened to coax my body to do unnatural things—like release you twenty weeks too early—rocked my soul.

When your perfect form emerged from the wreckage of my body, we were surrounded by our closest family and friends. A supernatural sense of peace filled the room, our family soon quietly excused themselves, and your mommy and daddy breathed in all the Lord made of you. We attempted to fit a lifetime of memories into a few short hours.

On November 24, in the dark of night, your daddy pulled around the car we purchased for bringing you home, physically picked me up out of the wheelchair because I could not stand on my own, set me gently into that car, and buckled me in like a child; we drove away from the hospital with empty arms and endless waves of tears. Instead of planning what our Thanksgiving feast would include, we planned the details of your funeral and what flowers would be at your burial.

Over the next year I played the hardest game in which I have ever participated: the blame game. I went back and forth casting the blame for your death upon myself—what I could have done or could have refrained from doing while carrying you—stressful circumstances, the Enemy, and even the ones I loved. At one point I was most confident I had found the culprit: the Enemy. I cursed him over and over. I am ashamed to say that I got so wrapped up in blaming that I was "giving" Satan power over not only your death but also my memories of your life. Those were such dark days without you, my precious girl, but there was one light that could shine even through the thick and scary depths of my pit. I finally decided I could no longer let your life and death bring so much pain.

I began seeking counsel from God's Word, our church leadership, and Hope Mommies, a non-profit organization started for mothers who have also experienced losses like mine. The Lord slowly began to chip away the scales that had hardened my heart. He opened my eyes, and I could push away the blame and instead let God reign over your life and death. You cannot imagine what a refreshing release that was for me, and I am so grateful you cannot know what it was like—you never felt pain, sorrow, loneliness, or grief. You were sweetly held your entire life, and when the Lord called you home, the first face you saw when you opened your eyes was his. I can only imagine.

That was the beginning of my journey to yearn for heaven like never before. God used you to spark a fire for him in my life in ways I did not know were possible. I was diving into a deeper relationship with him, but your absence was still all-consuming.

I constantly yearned for heaven to reunite with you, to know you. But desiring to be in your presence was overshadowing my desire to unite in glory with God Almighty. The sinful human nature is a sticky thing, and I constantly battle to desire what I can touch and feel less than what I imagine to come in eternity. Conviction is a beautiful gift; without it I would still idolize your absence in my life. It has been a bumpy journey, venturing through the ebbs and flows of hopeful grief. Some days are worse than others, but most days are woven with delightful hope over God's plans for me. He has entrusted me to steward your legacy to further his kingdom. When I look through those lenses, I am overcome with honor and a great weight of responsibility. You, Blair Reece, have helped me turn my blame game of "Why?" into "What now?" Instead of persistently coming to the feet of Jesus to request answers, I am gifted with the desire to throw my hopeful grief into action that stewards your legacy well. My prayer is that those actions will bring others closer to God.

The day we held you in our arms, our sweet nurse took pictures of you with a disposable camera. We also imprinted your hands and feet into our Bibles, dressed you in a tiny gown that swallowed you, kissed your lips, reveled at your beauty and God's design, counted your fingers and toes over and over, sang to you, told you all about your brothers and sisters, and then had to say, "See you later, baby girl." There are so many things I wish I could go back and do differently during those sacred hours, but I am so grateful for the memories we do have. Months after your delivery, I asked a friend to have the disposable camera developed for me. Much to my despair, the film ended up being damaged, and the only vision I have of you is what the Lord has burned into my memory. I pray every day that I will never forget what you look like. I have to giggle a little bit at my foolishness, considering you were delivered in an age of smartphones and top-notch technology. Grief does crazy things to the brain, and I guess part of my grief sent me back to the 1990s.

There are days when I feel that some people who do not understand look at you as a chance at life, and we just missed that "chance." But I want all to see your life as a special life—one we are greatly missing out on. I will miss your first tooth, your first step, your first skinned knee, your first day of school, your first fight with a friend, your first pair of ballet slippers (or would it have been cleats?), your first dance, your first date, your first mistake, your first pair of earrings, your first broken heart, your graduation, your first day of college, your wedding, your first day of work, your firstborn, your questions, the times you would have needed me, and the times I would have stayed up all night with worry over you. Because we missed out on all of your firsts, we will also miss out on all of your lasts, and everything in between. Even if I could, I would not want to take back any of what has happened. No matter how much your mommy misses you, sweet girl, I would never want to remove you from an eternity of perfection.

If you were here, your daddy would be so tender with you and want you to constantly know how well loved you are by him. Gavyn, your eldest brother, would constantly fuss over your safety and well-being—eldest child syndrome. Grant, brother number two, would make sure you had everything your heart desires.

Bertie, your biggest sister, would be your second mother with her nurturing spirit. Gwyneth, your feisty older sister, would teach you all aspects of being a princess and getting into trouble. Then there is Brynne Reece, the precious caboose that we named after you; she would most definitely pester you to no end. My heart always ponders the idea that if your precious life had not ended too soon, would hers even exist? Only God knows. You are so loved, and so is she.

While the days of missing you are long and the years are short, I will raise my hands and praise the one who gave me you. God gave me you and saw it best for his kingdom to have you home with him. God's plan for us earth-side is not necessarily to make me or any of his children comfortable; it is to make himself truly known, bring himself glory, and allow us an eternity in his presence. God used your perfectly planned life to open my eyes and my heart to this truth. The best is yet to come sweet girl; save mommy a seat. Because he lives, you live.

I love you,
Mommy

CHAPTER 10

Different Ways of Grieving

THE WAY MY HUSBAND GRIEVES IS DIFFERENT FROM THE WAY I GRIEVE

Two people were ready to welcome a daughter home. Two people were equally her parents. Two people were equally robbed by the thief, Stillbirth. Two people returned to an empty home, an empty crib, an empty room, and an empty-feeling life.

My husband wrote a letter to Noelle on April 21—four days after losing her in this life. While, of course, not knowing if he would ever share the letter with her, he did share it with me.

> Noelle, my love, how I miss you! So many tears have I shed, so much pain. What does life look like without you in it? For the past nine months I have never had to consider that. Yet now I am faced with questions no father should have to ask. *Why you, why now?* Would my pain be any less if I had answers to those questions? I do not believe so. You are my daughter. I love you too dearly for words. That will never change. And yet the question remains: how do I press on? How do I console

your grieving mother? How do I provide for us in the seeming monotony and trivialities of life when all I want to do is wake up from this bad dream, from the nightmare that has become our life, when it was supposed to be the sweetest dream of all? Oh Noelle, the questions are just too many. Yet seeing you was the bright spot in the darkness. Holding you in my arms filled my heart with solace. You have taught me so much about Jesus. I have learned more how to trust him, how to rely on him for not just my daily bread, but for the sustenance to take my next breath, plan my next thought, feel my next emotion. You have also taught me more of my heavenly Father's love as I received a father's heart. A heart that overflows with joy and pride in its child and breaks to see its child in pain. I have heard of many lives that yours has touched for eternity's sake by the grace of God, but none more deeply and significantly than your mother's and mine.

Two people were preparing to love her, and then, two people were living in the unimaginable.

And they were two different people.

I sat in my bed and on the sofa. I drew, thought, prayed, and read here and there. I wrote. I felt.

But he—he woke, he moved. He got dressed like he would have if she were here.

On our second day home from the hospital, he went to the kitchen to unload the dishwasher. I told him that he did not need to, but, no—he wanted to. At that moment, I could see where the temptation to disbelieve my husband's grief could enter into my mind and my heart. I could be tempted to question how someone could so quickly return to the simple patterns of life after losing someone so dear. But I recalled his face upon holding her. And I knew he was grieving the relationship he had with her as a father, the hopes and dreams he had formed for life with her. From that point on, sitting in bed without the remotest thought for the dishes, of all things, I told myself that his grief was different, and I welcomed it. What was farthest from my mind—I did not care what we ate from—was the opposite for him. And to keep him from his path forward, to disbelieve the grief I knew he was experiencing or to not recognize that in his heart he was doing those dishes *for me*, would have only diminished his God-exalting tribute.

He continued in the same trajectory: he went to the kitchen to prepare food I might have otherwise forgotten to eat. Early on, he drove me wherever I wanted to go in making preparations for her memorial service. He listened when I spoke—hearing every part of the storm of grief I relayed to him. And he sat by me when I cried. He sang and played guitar at her memorial service when I wanted no one else to do it. He continued to put forward his hands, head, and heart in service of the youth group at our church. He loved God and told them so. They knew it. Not a book, not a song, not a poem—to me, his most moving tribute was of a different kind.

There were days when he confessed that he felt somewhat purposeless, like he was growing weary of this world. And I knew it was because he could not serve Noelle like he was serving me and others. He would have been sweet with her, played with her for hours, fed her and helped her when she fell. I think there will continue to be impulses of his heart, mind, and hands intended just for her. I saw that God could not have given our daughter, Noelle, a better earthly father.

Later, my husband's tribute of service meant even more to me when I came to understand the faith in God it required. My husband's only child left this earthly life, and in the same day, his wife was thrust into an inexpressible grief. As a husband and as a father, he could do nothing about either. He could not bring Noelle back to us; he could not cure my tears. He could not snap her back; he could not snap me back. And, remarkably, he never attempted any remedies for either outside of his control. Instead, with all of that weight as a husband and father, he trusted the Lord. He left the weight with him. He entrusted his departed daughter to the Lord, and he entrusted his devastated wife to the Lord.

The letter to Noelle he wrote that day was not of his own initiative. He recorded it at my request, and I do not think it would be in existence otherwise. I might never have seen those words that ministered to and resonated with my soul out of his fatherly love for our daughter! He took steps forward with life readily and joyfully, as is his nature, but his grief was no less real for doing so. Both of us have our places in the purposes of God. Because I thought the best of him and his grief when tempted to do the opposite, I could be a joyful, encouraged onlooker of the fatherly tribute and commendable trust underpinning his much different way forward.

CHAPTER II

Feeling Fragile When Others Misunderstand My Grief

FEELING UNDERSTOOD AND VALUING OTHERS' UNDERSTANDING LESS

If I am a book, then different versions and translations of me seemingly exist everywhere. Acquaintances might read sentences, and friends may read paragraphs. Those very close to me might read nearly the whole of it. My book is now filled with pages darkened by loss and grief. Some misunderstand these words, leaving me feeling fragile. Others understand the words instantly because our pages are—in one way or another—similar. Yet, reading the versions, the translations, or even my very own copy are all different than having lived what those letters say. No other person in my life understands my letters like I do. Neither can I understand another's. The best we can do is be characters in and readers of each other's stories.

On this earth, if no one else understands me as deeply as I seek to be understood, then God must. And he does. God reads my book like no one else. He reads and understands. I am often tempted to think that Christianity is too good to be true. That there is a God who created me, loves me, sacrificed for me, and never leaves me seems too good.

Because I have been a born-again Christian since childhood, I can hardly read Psalm 139:1–6 like the words do not sound as familiar to me as the hands in my pockets.

> O Lord, you have searched me and known me!
> You know when I sit down and when I rise up;
>> you discern my thoughts from afar.
> You search out my path and my lying down
>> and are acquainted with all my ways.
> Even before a word is on my tongue,
>> behold, O Lord, you know it altogether.
> You hem me in, behind and before,
>> and lay your hand upon me.
> Such knowledge is too wonderful for me;
>> it is high; I cannot attain it.

King David, the psalm's author, and I seem to share a conclusion: these realities are too much to comprehend. They are too good to be true—but I need them to be true.

Though I wish God's hand upon me felt as familiar to me as my own, it does not. I forget that I am more familiar to him than he to me. Noelle has a mother on this earth who knows her, in part, and loves her. Though she could not see me, and never fully met me, my love and knowledge of her is no less true—of that I am certain. How much more certain is God's knowledge of me, though I have not seen him!

He searches each corner of me and knows all of me in a simple act of knowledge. He knows every action and move. He knows the thoughts that pass and the thoughts that burn in my heart. He knows the thoughts that need to be expressed and the thoughts that have hardly been expressed. He knows the thoughts that keep me awake at night and the thoughts that circulate within throughout my day.

He knows my ways—how I like when people tell me about how they miss, love, and will remember Noelle, while I do not care as much when people tell me they have sorrow for me. He knows the words on my tongue. He knows that I appreciate all who have approached me to "say something," for all have been caring. He knows my feelings. He knows that I express understanding for those who do not know exactly what to say in the moment. He knows that I mean it too.

And just when someone close enough speaks one phrase that is too insensitive too soon, he hems me behind and before so that— though the words make me feel fragile—I am not left without support. The words do not crush me. When I think about how to answer the comment I hoped I would not have to hear, I feel him again, the weight of his hand upon me. When a remark opens the hole of grief in me, I come to know again that God is larger still. His hand abundantly covers. It is too wonderful. But it is true.

He is the grand author of this world who, without being the author of evil, writes the words on my pages. He reads them attentively. He understands them intuitively. He authors me gently. He cares about me and knows me such that the pain of others' misunderstanding does not devastate or shake. What is too wonderful for me is actually and truly mine—a prelude to a hurtless heaven. I feel it now: he gets me.

Pastor and Bible scholar S. Lewis Johnson teaches,

> The concept of a personal and gracious Father negates any notion of stoic resignation, distance, or apathy. The transcendent

God of eternity is also the immanent God for every believer, in the person of Jesus Christ. Every hour and minute, God personally superintends the life of every believer, even when they are hurting and suffering. [...] The God of eternity becomes the God of the hour for each of his saints when they become the recipients of his providential care and concern.[1]

Who is this God of eternity? There is another element to consider concerning my story: my capacities for understanding him. To appreciate what it means that he reads me, understands me, and authors me, I need knowledge of him—about the heart and mind that invented mine.

Upon further thought, I am surprised to remember that he does not actually have a heart or a mind—those are human components. Ascribing a heart or mind to God is a figure of speech, an anthropomorphism. The truths they communicate about God's character are accurate; still, they are merely pictures, figures, not full descriptions. I have very few sentences about God that do not contain figures. He is so far beyond me.

I think about some of the other ways that he can be truly, yet not fully, described. He is Creator, Master, the Trinity, transcendent, immanent, sovereign, just, righteous, holy, omniscient, omnipotent, immutable, veracious, self-existent, eternal, and more. There are lifetimes and lifetimes, unending, of depth to know and learn. Lifetimes spent in awe.

I think about Scripture, the whole of it as his self-revealed, flawless Word. It contains his plan for this world. And as I grow in my understanding of this book, I see that I can also stay extremely confident that he will execute his plan for this world in order that good will come from all of my pages and letters. He will be glorified for who he is—his creation will know him and praise him.

He is not seeking or needing my permission to do this work, but to see this all become true will be the greatest pleasure of my life. Preacher D. Martyn Lloyd Jones teaches,

> What is the will of God? It is the final ground of everything, of all existence. It is the final explanation of everything that has ever happened or everything that will happen. And the Bible teaches that the will of God is sovereign; in other words, it is not determined by anything but by God Himself. It is the expression of His Lordship, His absolute being.
>
> But remember, His will is never arbitrary. It is never exercised except in perfect harmony with all the other attributes of God's great and glorious being. It is the same God who is omniscient, who is omnipresent. It is the same God who is glorious and wonderful. It is the same God who is love and compassion and mercy. We must not divide these things, though we distinguish them for the purposes of thought and understanding.[2]

So, when I take a step back, even for a short amount of time, in order to try to understand this Person who is reading, understanding, and yes, even authoring my book, I see that there is indescribable joy. For the God who is glorious and beyond me understands me; the God who is a divine wealth of a sovereign Person authors me; and the God who masterfully plans all of history is compassionately taking these pages of grief and bending each and every word towards the purposes of his glory.

I yearn to be understood. Yet, through turning my eyes up, seeing the Person whose caring hand rests upon me, I am changed. I find that being understood is second to understanding more of him—yes, much more satisfying and significant is dwelling upon and seeking to better understand the Person who has already understood me completely. If I am a book with pages of grief, he reads each word. If I am a book with pages of grief, he understands it all. If I am a book—even through each page, paragraph, and letter—oh, that I may contribute, in some way, to *his* story! Let me know him; let me be his.

One Year Closer

Stephanie Blanks

I knew it was coming: the third of each month had been a marker, reminding me of the worst day of my life. Except, the third of February would not only be a reminder. It would be the day—my dark day. On February 3, I would stop counting the months. From then on, I would measure time since the last day I held Kinley in years.

This day scared me. I did not know what this day would look like or how I would handle it. One year seemed so permanent. Month markers, although hard, still meant that the last time I held my daughter was very recent. But this would be the first anniversary of her death; I had been separated from my precious girl for an entire year.

For some, a baby's birthday and death day are the same. For me, February 3 would only be her death day. Kinley's birthday was forty-four days earlier. My daughter was born with a brain malformation and never breathed on her own. She stayed in the neo-natal intensive care unit for forty-four days before she died. On this day, there would be no celebration of her life. No pink cupcakes or birthday song that had been present on her birthday. This day would only mark death.

But God, in his infinite mercy, had other plans for this day. Instead of the despair I had dreaded, he ushered in hope. Sorrow was comforted by peace. God cast light that overpowered darkness. I woke up on February 3 full of memories—but not painful ones.

I remembered the support God had given to us through family and friends. I thought about how my best friend had checked in with me daily to see how I was doing. I reflected on how our Sunday school class had planted a tree in Kinley's honor. I pondered all of the ways our family had served us through meals, childcare, and housework. I cherished the cards and gifts other grieving mothers had sent to me. I marveled at how an anonymous, generous soul had paid for Kinley's funeral. I thought of how my love for my husband deepened because of the way our baby girl had bonded us. The hands of God were at work the entire year comforting me, cradling me, and reassuring me that I was going to be okay. But most of all, on February 3 I was reminded of the hope of seeing my beautiful daughter again.

Here are some of the personal reflections I recorded that day.

One year ago today, our beautiful daughter was called home after spending only forty-four days on earth. Kinley's death caused me to question the goodness of God. Here is some of what I have learned: we are stewards of the gifts he gives us, and Kinley was a precious gift on loan for a very short time. Joy and sorrow walk hand in hand. I saw this in my daughter's life, and we see this in the life of Jesus. If his story had ended with death, God could not have been good. But it did not! It began again with new life and the offer of an eternity in heaven available to us all. That is the life Kinley is experiencing. I miss her so much, but I rejoice for her. Even in pain, God is still good. In fact, he is great.

That peace, that gratefulness for who God is and how he has blessed my life, even in tragedy, could only come from him. I could not have achieved it on my own, and no human person could have bestowed it upon me. This is not to say that I did not feel any sorrow on February 3. Believe me, grief was still present, but it did not conquer me. I had changed my focus; it was not her "death day," but became to me her "heaven day."

Seven years later, there are still tears, and the ache for my daughter will remain with me every day until I see her again. How could I not miss her? But to think that Kinley has been in the presence of Jesus for seven years—that makes me smile! I picture my girl with Jesus and how all she knows is joy. February 3 is not defined by death. It marks the first day of Kinley's eternal life, and for that, I can rejoice.

CHAPTER 12

Physical, Cyclical Grief

COMING TO TERMS WITH MY GRIEVING PROCESS

Knowing that God comforts and understands, knowing that I was not leaving my daughter behind by moving forward through grief, and knowing that he would eventually bring me to new purposes all enabled me to ask new questions: *Would my bogged-down mind ever return to normal, and would I ever feel bodily strength again?*

The emotional and mental weight of the loss occupied so much of my thoughts that my mind seemed only good for floating in the storm clouds. I felt as though my feet could not reach the ground from being swept upward into the high storm. It was not gentle and not like a dream; the storm was violent. So, my body felt its bruise.

I heard "cries" of the storm—like theological questions needing resolution, tears needing to be released, or new life decisions needing to be made. To resolve a cry of the storm, I needed to "answer" it—with theological resolution found through Scripture, an experience of relating with others that allowed my tears to be expressed, or a decision made about a next step of life. Over time, the storm became less and less deafening, until one day I found that the pain of loss no longer kept me from movement and life.

At the beginning of my grief, I was not even capable of mentally walking. The pitch of the storm was nearly deafening. I began to answer the cries of the storm one-by-one as they came. And while I did, I became better and better at denying any counter-shouts of specific expectations for how quickly the clouds should be clearing—whether self-expectation or expectations from others. Instead, I leaned into my own individual process of grief. I learned to ache and sink with my bruises into each next step of grief until I could, for example, express my sorrow again or relate to someone else's grief. Either option would release some sorrow and clear some of the storm. When I did, my feet felt more confident in walking again.

As I progressed through my grief, I began to think of it less like a storm and more like a multilevel spiral. The spiral began high above the routines of life, above what used to feel like normalcy. From the top, I could not see the ground. But I came to learn there were levels to the spiral, platforms where I could rest my feet for a time. Each time I traveled from one level to the next, I felt a sense of relief and resolution. To travel again down the spiral at each new level of grief, I needed to relieve some of my sorrow. I would, for example, examine all of the pieces of the time I had with my daughter to gain a sense of release from some of the grief. In a sermon on grief, my pastor, Colin Smith, gave this insight into this practice.

> Imagine a priceless vase or ornament is dropped on the floor and smashed to pieces. The woman who loved it kneels

down. She picks up the pieces, one by one. She looks at each one in detail, turning it round, as if to remember where it once belonged.

The vase was loved and so when it was shattered, every piece was worth picking up, no matter how small. A grieving person will often want to talk about the smallest detail of their loss. It is as if every broken piece is taken up and wept over. When you listen, you may feel that the detail was small, but it is part of something that was supremely valued, part of something dearly loved.[1]

When, through examining the pieces of my grief and life with my daughter, I reached the next platform, I also found a new experience of the same grief, the same loss. Some parts of the spiral were not necessarily emotions or recollections. They were new decisions or truths to love. But whichever the case, grief was still present on each new level toward the ground. It was a spiral downward; the grief felt cyclical. It brought me around to the same type of place, though different. I was going through the same emotional sorrows, the same loss in different phases. But, thankfully, I was traveling toward the ground—whether I could see it or not.[2]

To combine the two images now, I imagined a multilevel spiral coming down through a storm cloud. The cloud was a bruising one. But it was one that dissipated as the ground neared. At each platform along the spiral, a new sightline toward the ground gave hope. At the end of the spiral's swirl, I hoped to be able to walk again on the ground because I had feebly practiced walking through the storm when discovering each next release of grief.

Grieving is work. It is not a time of mere rest when activity stops; in my experience, it is time to pray, read Scripture, read some books, and remember. And it is a time to do all of that while being fully in the moment, crying tears, writing favorite memories, praying for those on the journey who experienced a similar loss, discovering the ways to express what is felt, seeking biblical answers to questions, and allowing oneself to be restored.

Initially, I found the idea of working outside the home difficult primarily because I had not planned to do so once my daughter arrived. I was resistant. Yet, I somehow grieved through that resistance, coming to understand that were I to do nothing but what I would have done were my daughter with me, I would not have much to do. I resonated with a new truth. I answered the storm's cry. Then, I slid one circle down that spiral and put my feet on new ground, a new level. I was able to return to work—*progress*.

I came to a new level closer to normalcy—one level closer to the real thing, the real ground—and yet, it was also a new level of the storm. Working was a new reality of life to navigate without my daughter. I was unclouded from the grief that kept me from working outside the home, but then, there was another aspect of grieving to do that I could only see with newly unclouded eyes. Working brought its own new storm-cries, requiring new relief. Were I to enumerate each cry and each part of the spiral, this book would become very long.

There were many parts of the spiral, both big and small. I later answered one big cry by moving away from the home where I had prepared to welcome my daughter. There, I had created her nursery and playroom while pregnant. So much of her memory was there. At an early point, I wanted to leave it all in order to escape the sorrow, and then, at another point, I wanted to never separate myself from it. Neither allowed me to reach a new level of normalcy. I grieved through those periods too; I found my next way down the spiral and moved to a new home. I gained new ground to move forward upon—literally and figuratively.

Through the repetition of cyclical grief, two themes repeated with each stage of progress. First, when one cloudy level of grief cleared, and I traveled one more loop down to reach a new platform, I was able to look above me to see more truths and comforts than I previously could. Second, participating in grief and continuing to travel down each of its stages did nothing to diminish my love for my daughter.

Writing these words, I live in a new home, still doing the new job I started some time ago. As I look at the new ground I have reached, I have the same experience. I miss her again, anew. This new home has only one bedroom; there is no place for her. There is not a room for her because it was not needed. Yet, I feel it freshly—even without needing a room, there will always be a place for her with us.

Later, as I began to consider that I might be past the cycle of grief—such that my life contained grief but was not characterized by it—I was hit with a new memory. I sat in a seminary class for the first time since losing my girl. I sat, and I sank with weakness while feeling bruised by the storm clouds' familiar ache. I knew by then how to recognize grief. The physical ache told me that there was a cry I needed to somehow answer.

Never could I have imagined myself sitting in class while being a mom; it was not the plan. Instead, I hoped to transfer my existing credits toward an online degree. Cyclical with repeating kinds of feelings, with physical ramifications in being bruised, being cloudy in not seeing my own way, and including feebleness in learning how to walk in normalcy—yet, with progress—this was my grief.

I have needed two kinds of hope in grief. So far, I have written about the otherworldly hope. I will never stop needing it, of course. But that otherworldly hope started to give me a hope about life on earth, the life to which God was faithfully returning me. If he could bear the weight of one day making all things new, surely he could renew me fully for this life too. If he was really ahead there, having prepared a place for me and my daughter, was he not also really here, living within me too and restoring me to this life?

Does grief end? I have tried to answer from my own heart and realized that I do not know how. But five years after my loss, sitting to edit what I wrote within the year or so after my daughter's loss, I think the truth is something close to this: I will never stop grieving the loss of my daughter who lives ahead, but the initial storm of the grief no longer keeps me from living fully here. I am more deeply motivated for living well here because I so thoroughly believe in and love heaven. And I will never stop missing my daughter here, but as time progresses, I think of her predominantly, even nearly exclusively in heaven—and, in that, I am overtaken by joy.

Life has become characterized by moving forward and walking instead of by finding the way down. God has been faithful to make me walk again. I was thrust into a storm. Each part of the spiral passed to a new level of normalcy until he returned me to the ground made for moving forward. But I had to take my time learning to walk again.

I still walk with faith that he will show me the way back down to living on this earth when the storm, over the course of my life, might swirl me up again for a brief time. And I do have faith; for when I look up at each level of the spiral traveled and cloud dissipated, I see evidence of a God who cloud-cleared a howling storm when I could scarcely see one next step.

Physical, Cyclical Grief

The heart of man plans his way,
but the LORD establishes his steps.
—Proverbs 16:9

CHAPTER 13

My Loss, My Baby's Gain

THE JOY OF REMEMBERING THE SENSE OF
BELONGING MY BABY HAS GAINED

My husband and I moved to a new ground of grief by moving to a different home—a fresh apartment in Lincoln Park, Chicago, after living in the suburbs for years. We moved from the place where our daughter's nursery and playroom were created, each detail and decoration determined with care. Baby shower presents arrived at the front door of that home. The surrounding coffee shops were utilized for their decaffeinated option, a departure for me at the time. The route to the doctor's office was memorized, each trip containing a seemingly new level of pregnancy-exacerbated carsickness. The place was full of her. It was made full for her.

She had traded one fullness for a better one.

I, on the other hand, was given emptiness for fullness. My husband and I did not leave the first home we built together for over a year after Noelle's death. I did not want to move to escape it. It held memories, memories I wanted to treat well. We left to move forward because we were able and desiring. To live in a new home was one way to continue to step forward into our new reality: we no longer had her here. A cloud cleared for me through this move.

My husband and I moved to a neighborhood in which we hardly knew anyone and where hardly anyone knew us. Adventure was possible—in the new places we could discover and explore—especially being in downtown Chicago, close to Lake Michigan and its beach, the largest farmers' market I had ever seen, and neighborhood shops with interesting finds I could stow away for our tiny attic apartment.

As I write this, I recall how, maybe a few years ago, the idea of moving somewhere different from where I had been living in order to create a new self might have appealed to me, but no longer. Now, I would lose far too much were I wanting to reinvent myself: the experiences I have had, the people I have known, and the precious daughter I have lovingly carried have all made me. They have all been the tools God used to form me—my character, thoughts, and heart.

From our new home, we traveled back north to visit family, and we traveled to visit friends too. Among our friends and family, we felt a fullness that I had not yet felt in my new neighborhood. People knew me because they shared our memories and lives. Park benches, a raspberry-picking farm, small and still lakes—we shared places too. These people understood me. They understood not because I told them about myself in a conversation—like when introducing myself to people at a different church for the first time—but because they were present with me in my past. That fullness of shared experiences and places felt familiar and safe.

In part, I think of heaven similarly. God is full and complete in himself, with no need for people. But in heaven, he invites people to participate in his fullness as adopted sons and daughters. From his fullness, I have received this grace. Because of what he has done, heaven will contain for me the fullness of joy. Jesus came so that I might have life to the full (Jn. 10:10). I suspect I hold empty places with weaknesses and inadequacies that I do not even know need his filling, but in heaven, I will be known and understood. I will see him working in all of my past, ordaining it. In heaven, I will see God in all of his fullness. And I will see with piercing clarity that he has always been enough for me. This heavenly place is where I will feel understood, where I will feel my soul click, unlike anywhere else.

This place will hold the union of a Christ to his bride. Yet, more than a union, it will be a reunion in which his people will see that God was faithfully, intimately present on earth. When sitting at the table of celebration and consummation with him, I will sit at a chair whose welcoming seat I have not earned by my own merit. Yet, I will know the seat to be so surely mine—there could be no other space I would want to fill in all of creation. I will be in his fullness. I will belong.

The fullness I will feel, of familiarity and belonging, is the fullness of who he is to me. Only the fullness of God could possibly make each unique person feel as though he or she belongs. When I do, when I finally feel it—entire belonging to a perfect Lord—I will start my joy through the endless ages. I will see new light upon new light about all he has done for me and who he is. For his fullness is gloriously weighty—a glory that belongs to him rightfully and only. I will be satisfied. I will know what it is to uninhibitedly attribute my fulfillment to him—to glorify him in every task, job, and endeavor.

As earthly life is known for needs, so heavenly life will be known for fulfillment. Earth is known for a certain emptiness, a toil, that accompanies daily, mundane life. I might ask myself, *Is this really going to be worth it in the end?* There will be no toil in heaven. That place already sounds like home, the home for which I have been created—where every task I do will not only feel meaningful but will *be* meaningful. Each activity will be used to reflect another aspect of who he is, through which I will repeatedly tell him and others just how glorious he is.

So, life eternal—which is really him—will, with perfect, all-seeing eyes, perceive the different forms of emptiness I could have, the needs that could ache and burn within me, and it will overtake them. Eternal life is larger; it is more dominant than my needs and knows exactly how to make them disappear. Being larger than me, eternity will overtake me, but not as something powerful that seeks only to control and eventually dismiss once its purposes are complete. It will consume me and take me up like a rush of rejoicing, with many running together there. No one will fear being lost or cast aside by the many. It will swallow me, yes. Yet, in the swallowing I will not be hurt. I will be welcomed into that which is larger than who I am, and indeed, larger than my needs and shortcomings. Out of that which is larger, which overtakes, swallows, and consumes, I will find myself remade to be able to bear glory.

Everything that I have and am and have done will be purposed for his glory. To think of reinventing myself or forgetting those ways he formed me on earth—near suburban raspberry farm or skyscraper-lined farmers' market—will not be. I will remember what it was to be empty, breathless, toiling, and pained. Each lacking earthly memory will be redeemed and will point to a characteristic of who he is—merciful, gracious, faithful, etc.—that I could have never otherwise known in the same way. And each recollection of life on this earth will be a remembrance of what I deserve—damnation—from which I will have been fully saved.

The lacking earthly experiences, even the sinful ones, will tell me over and over that I could have never accomplished for myself what he has. I will not be glad for the sins, but only glad for the Redeemer I better know him to be. Earthly experiences will tell me that, surely, only he is good.

Prior to losing my daughter, I anticipated her many firsts—a first smile, step, and word. But I did not expect that she would experience a first that I still await. Of us, she was first to meet our Lord. As a mother, it does not seem that my own little baby should go much of anywhere without me, much less be first to do something that is still incomprehensible to me on earth. Whatever she had to do and wherever she had to go in life, I had hoped to "be there" for her. But I could not be there for her in death. I could not go with her. I could not tell her what to expect. I could not help her through. But Jesus could. And I have the hope that Jesus did.

Though I feel that I lack my daughter right now, she does not lack me because she is in the place where there is no lacking. I believe that because she is in the place of perfection, fully seeing and knowing (1 Cor. 13:12), she is not doing what other babies would on this earth. Instead of having tummy time, learning to smile, and starting to recognize the people in her life, she is, even now (Lk. 23:43), beyond the earthly me in knowledge and wisdom. She is full. She has been swallowed up by the Lord Jesus Christ, the Life, in God's heaven. In every place I know yearning, she knows the fullness of God.

When the new heaven and new earth are established, God's filling presence will be forever established as dwelling with his people: "And I heard a loud voice from the throne saying, 'Behold, the dwelling place of God is with man. He will dwell with them, and they will be his people, and God himself will be with them as their God'" (Rev. 21:3).

Writing on these verses, commentator Matthew Henry reflects:

> *They shall be his people;* their souls shall be assimilated to him, filled with all the love, honour, and delight in God which their relation to him requires, and this will constitute their perfect holiness; and he will be their God: *God himself will be their God;* his immediate presence with them, his love fully manifested to them, and his glory put upon them, will be their perfect happiness; then he will fully answer the character of the relation on his part, as they shall do on their part.[1]

When I think of all of this—and the longing I have for this place of glory and love with the Lord—I feel as much as I can the completion of it all for her. This experience has been my loss, and I am bereft of both giving my daughter belonging and experiencing my belonging with her. But to be with this God so soon has been my dear daughter's incomparable gain.

THREE YEARS CLOSER

Brittnie Blackburn

A little over three years have passed since I said hello and goodbye to my only son, Chance. Three years had an odd way of feeling like thirteen years, and at the same time, three hours. How was it possible that only three years ago I sat in hospital room 307 and held my tiny, beautifully formed boy in my arms?

There had been no concerns; this pregnancy seemed no different than my others. Yet at my twenty-week anatomy scan I learned that my son no longer had a beating heart. Two days later, I was induced, and at 4:49 p.m. on Saturday, April 4, I pushed my little boy out of my body. I spent five hours holding him, studying his face as to never forget his features. Watching the nurse walk out of the hospital room with him later that evening was the most gut-wrenching moment of my life. Recalling that moment still brings tears to my eyes.

Two days after his birth, we honored his life, surrounded by our family and friends. All who came dressed in bold, bright colors and carried blue balloons. And then, we laid Chance in the ground and walked away, starting a new life without him.

The months that followed were some of the darkest and hardest of my life. I trusted God fully and felt no anger towards him. Yet I began to experience symptoms I now know to be common of sudden loss: insomnia, anxiety, irritability, and the inability to make even the simplest of decisions. Feelings of loneliness, vivid dreams, and a preoccupation with death and dying were also my reality.

Riding the waves of grief was not a pretty experience. Yet with the passing of time, by letting myself feel any emotion that came, and through hours clocked in a biblical counselor's office, I emerged on the other side. God was so gracious to walk with me each step of the way. Through all the questioning and tears, he was there.

Time is proving that this journey of love and loss has not been wasted. For this I am beyond thankful. Through the loss of Chance, God has renewed my faith, hope, and trust—and opened my eyes and my family's eyes to his heavenly tapestry being woven through our story.

The phrase "everything happens for a reason," does not sit well with me when it is arbitrarily said and not connected with the God of the Bible, but the Bible does teach that purpose can be brought from everything that happens to his people (Rom. 8:28). If I disagree with God about that, what is my alternative? To remain bitter and forever identified by my losses? That is not how I want to live.

I choose purpose.

I think of Chance every single day. When I think of my son, I think of the promise of heaven, and when I think of heaven, I think of my Savior, Jesus. Chance's life renews my focus on the only one I actually need: Jesus. When I think of Chance, I am reminded to keep looking up, instead of side-to-side, knowing that anything I will ever need has been given to me through the day Jesus gave himself on the cross. Thanks to my son, my mind is pointed to Jesus daily, sometimes even hourly. That is purpose.

Losing Chance has also given me the courage to continually share the truth of the gospel because I know life does not end with death. If I know such a "secret" the world does not know without being told (Rom. 10:14), how can I not share it? That is purpose.

Losing Chance has given me credibility with a hurting world. Struggling souls hear my story and see my life, and all the while, I demonstrate to them God's sufficiency to meet my needs. Chance's life and story has opened the door for connection; this experience has offered light for understanding and speaking into others' darkness. My family loved and lost, but we have not lost hope. We still have joy. We do not despair. This speaks volumes to those in pain who do not know the Lord. God has blessed our lives through Chance so that we can be a blessing to others. That is purpose.

Losing Chance heightened my awareness of all the gifts in my life. I became more attuned to the good, the blessings. All the things that, had I not lost my son, I could more easily take for granted: the roof over my head, food on my table, water in my faucet, my living children, my husband who works endlessly to support my family, the pink rose bush that sits outside my front window. Now, when I ponder these blessings, my mind turns to praise. My son reminds me that there is much good, much to be grateful for—and that it matters to stop and worship the Lord in thankfulness. That is purpose.

Losing Chance and getting to the other side of grief has renewed my trust in God's faithfulness. I know hard times will come again—that is an earthly guarantee—yet by remembering God's grace and faithfulness in carrying my family through the loss of Chance, I will more clearly be able to face the next hurdle, challenge, or loss. This is the pattern God uses to grow and stretch me and renew my faith. I remember and look back in order to look ahead, and I remind myself that his faithfulness has indeed been my strength. He has brought me through so much already, and he will continue to bring me through. That is purpose.

While I do not believe God is glad I grieve, I do believe he allowed it to happen for my good and his glory—for his greater purposes. While this belief does not remove suffering or instantly heal the hurt, it does redeem it.

Would I love to be together with my son? Absolutely. Do tears pool in my eyes from time to time, even three years later, as I think of what could have been? Absolutely. Images fill my mind, such as Chance running around making messes or starting preschool or crying once again about greens on his dinner plate. Without a doubt these moments come to me and take my breath away. Yet God has extended his hand and used the gentle passing of time to open my eyes to the ways in which he is using pain to impact eternity.

Gratitude fills my heart as I reflect on the lessons three years have uncovered. I thank God for giving me my only son, Chance Michael, if even for a mere twenty weeks in my womb. I remember that God is always working and bringing purpose; and I acknowledge that my time on this earth is but for a moment, and in the blink of an eye, I will be reunited with my son once more.

For now, I am three years closer, three years stronger in the knowledge of God's faithfulness, and have never been more hopeful. God does not waste a moment of my pain. He brings purpose.

CHAPTER 14

My Baby is a Child of God

Perhaps my baby is somewhat like an angel in that she never chose sin. But yet, my baby is not an angel literally—and especially not symbolically in the sense of what my culture thinks of angels. But the idea is tempting.

When my daughter lay spiritless in a body that no longer supported life, she looked of death, reflecting neither who she would have been on earth nor who she is now in heaven. She smelled like she was not alive, and her lips had changed. I still refrain when describing death's effects upon her—not wanting to detail them in full. Her face became less and less round. She hardly resembled herself as the minutes wore on. Old Testament scholar Walter Kaiser quoted an early church father, Lactantius, in his book on Lamentations: "No one can love life without abhorring death; and no one can have an appetency for light, without an antipathy to darkness."[1]

For nine months, everything within me was geared toward the birth of a new, beautiful baby who would smell soft and sweet. Her eyes would peek open, though sleepily and not entirely at first. She would be full. She would be only alive. My baby was a person all of my family and friends would soon meet. My husband and I anticipated showing them a new, unique personality of whom observations could be made right away—whose traits among the family might she resemble? But when my baby was born, all of my expectations were left unmet.

No personality was present for me to observe, and I am left to guess based on my short time with her who she might have been. Though I have ideas from her life in my womb and her facial features, what she might be like, I cannot confirm them. A new, unique person entered our lives—a new creation of God—though no one was able to meet her.

Immediately after my experience with death, the doctor told me that my baby was an angel in heaven—a sweet, wise, winsome, doe-eyed angel. The vivid, present mental image that is conjured by the term angel—however inaccurate of biblical angels—is certainly closer to the one that I had in mind for nine months than having no person to show and only images of her that were covered with death.

I desperately needed comfort. I had hardly contemplated my own death, much less that of my child. I did not know from where to exactly derive this comfort, for the Bible suddenly seemed very big and broad. I did not know where to start. I had the energy to read one paragraph, perhaps, but not to discern the right one. And all of my being knew exactly how to ache for my baby more than it remembered how to ache for Jesus in the beginning of grief.

I remember that the doctor told me that my baby was an angel in heaven—a protective, guardian angel. I was certainly in need of comfort, and my baby was already so dominating of my thoughts that, really, the idea of my baby protecting me sounded appealing.

Later, my mind replayed news articles I had seen about abortion, and a new one also came across my sight. In it, a leading woman representing Planned Parenthood stated that her child's personhood was initiated the moment that child was born and not before. Many other articles condoned abortion in various ways. I felt that I could not possibly be more repulsed by any notions of the human mind. When I read of so many people seeking to protect the ability to end preborn life, after my daughter was stillborn, I understand even less why anyone would be leery of attributing the word murder to it.

Allow me to pause for a moment. Whenever or wherever I write about abortion, I feel compelled to write to the many mothers and fathers who have survived their babies gone by the decision for abortion. There is hope, there is forgiveness, there is mercy, there is freedom. These are found in the powerful abundance of who Jesus Christ is and what he has done. And I say this with a further qualifying statement—though I have not experienced the personal trauma and sin of abortion, I do know, as a person who would have no hope for forgiveness without Christ for my personal, heinous offenses, Christ gives an abundance of mercy and freedom to those who place their trust in him. For followers of Christ who believe in him as their Lord for the forgiveness of their sins—based upon his atoning sacrifice in their place—there is now no condemnation (Rom. 8:1). That is the good news.

After reading those articles, I recalled the doctor telling me that my baby is other-worldly, an angel in heaven. An angel is a being with obvious value. The perception of an angel's worth is, perhaps, more than that of a human. As a mother, I long for my child's life and personhood to be valued. I do not seek her personhood to be more valued than another's; and certainly, there is no less value in my child's life and personhood than the rest of mankind. But yet, the status of my baby feels so diminished by my culture that, yes, she is angelic by comparison. After all, the group to which she belongs has been so very marginalized that a portion of the U.S. population would resonate with the notion that those in her category and situation (unborn for all of earthly life) were never people at all.

I want to think of her as she would have been if she were still here: my daughter. She is a daughter who would have grown into her own—a beloved member of our family. She is significant because she was made to be human by God; all people are significant because they were made to be his humans.

My baby is not an angel. The truth is far better.

For now, I have lost the opportunity to learn the unique personality of my child, to see her grow, to introduce her to friends and family. Though I do not yet know who my baby is, I have the comfort of knowing that her personality has not disappeared or faded. I have a Good Shepherd who cares for the individual—who knows his own and calls his own by name (Jn. 10:3). On this earth, I feel like the preserver of my daughter's memory. But I can trust that God is more concerned than I am about my daughter's unique personality and nature. He created her, and his bond with her is older and closer than mine. She belonged to him before she belonged with me.

Though when I saw her last she wore the death I hate, I will one day see her with a resurrected body. "The body that is sown is perishable, it is raised imperishable; it is sown in dishonor, it is raised in glory; it is sown in weakness, it is raised in power; it is sown a natural body, it is raised a spiritual body" (1 Cor. 15:42–44 NIV). Earthly bodies are perishable. I know it better than I want to know it. But, my baby's body will resurrect to be indestructible. Earthly bodies are those capable of sin. But one day, my baby's body will be a glorified body in which sin will not be a possibility. Earthly bodies are carriers of the consequences of sin. My baby's body will have the power of life that Christ imparts such that death can never swallow her again. I have known what it is for death to swallow my own baby's body, but I will sing loudly on that resurrection day, "Death has been swallowed up in victory" (1 Cor. 15:54 NIV). More reassuring than being an angel is that my daughter—body, personhood, spirit, soul, mind, will, memory, and future—is uniquely in the care of her heavenly Father.

I too am in the protective care of my Father. As the sovereign King whose purposes can never be thwarted and a Good Shepherd who laid his life down for his sheep, I have the assurance that he is my best caregiver. Not only does he know my baby by name, he knows me by name. With my baby as a guardian, I would have no solid answers: *Does she see me from where she resides? Does she have power to care for me? Does she have the ability to influence my heart in this world such that I am protected?*

There are no answers to these questions as it concerns my child, only because God has already given me himself. This is the gospel. Jesus Christ—fully man and fully God—was on earth in the form of a human, knowing all of my limitations, and he gave his life for me. He succeeded in earning life, for he was raised from and for the dead. He sees me now and intercedes for my unique needs. He directs all situations and events for his greater purposes that I can trust; all authority has been given to him (Matt. 28:18). He influences my life and heart for good. He gives me the pleasure of knowing him and bringing him glory. I have him—his comfort, his presence, his intercessions, his sovereign control of my life, his hope for my baby, his hope for me, and his promise that sorrow is not the end of my experience as a person. I have his spiritual rebirth for my daughter when her first birth did not turn out as expected. And I have his rebirth in me. I can lean on it all as my comfort. This knowledge, unlike any human thought, is secure because he is my solid foundation for truth, the Rock: "Lead me to the rock that is higher than I" (Ps. 61:2).

From this worldview, I have all reason to be certain that my baby's personhood started at conception. In fact, my life shouts it. I have announced, planned, posted, photographed, mused, grown, purchased, waited, smiled, and dreamed. No written text tells me more boldly than Scripture that not only did my baby's personhood and life begin in the womb, but so did mine. I was knit nowhere else and found my beginnings nowhere but there (Ps. 139:13). Who else was I from the beginning if not myself? No one to whom God has given his image (Gen. 1:27) could possibly be devalued. Human thoughts and words cannot disrupt the plans of God.

In some ways, God's image upon man seems mysterious to me (Gen. 1:27). Yet, I know that when I look at others, I see God's character imparted in small ways across the population. Though never to be confused with God, I reflect him to others, and they reflect him to me—and all back to him, made to be ambassadors of him. All people are in his image—my baby no less so. This stamp of value from the hand of God cannot be wiped away. So, that which comes from the mighty, eternal Word of the living God cannot be disrupted by the breath of someone whose life, by virtue of being human, is itself a mere breath. Christ is strong enough to bear the weight of all of my hopes.

All have different gifts—often beautifully employed after loss. Some have messages. Some have care groups. Some have blog posts. Some have books. Some have more children to tell of the joys of heaven. Some have friends who now have a way to feel understood. Some have unique, understanding prayers that can now be spoken. Some have listening ears. The list continues. As C. S. Lewis wrote, pain can be used as a "megaphone to rouse a deaf world."[2] Yet, my baby's worth has already been established— the same worth all people share. No audience or giftedness can tell the world how to value my daughter more than God has already told the world how to value her as a person in his eternal Word.

My baby is not an angel—not even symbolically. But she is imperishable, to be raised in glory and power, uniquely known and loved by the God who calls her by name, a reflection to me of the image of God, possessing value that no human breath can dispel, and maintaining an equal value to all other babies and children who have ever been lost or who have ever been. I am one also loved by God, who called me by name to know him personally, who has the very presence of God in this life, and will certainly be ushered into life that will never perish or fade. This list of my daughter's realities and mine is better to me than any other list that I could imagine.

CHAPTER 15

My Longings

A STEWARDSHIP ENNOBLED
THROUGH DIVINE ASSOCIATION

Noelle and I shared a life-altering experience. I felt we were drawn near as her earthly life ended within me and my body carried her death. So, to venture into recollection of my loss was also to revisit my bond with her. If I could not join her through death, I felt I could still "join" her in the magnitude of my sorrow over our last moments together. Once, I was resistant toward releasing my sorrow for fear of losing nearness with her, causing my heart to bloat with unexpressed tears—but, in time, I learned that God would immeasurably absorb my flood.

After that, my heart was still raw with pure longing—to be with her. Had sin not entered our world, my arms would be holding my daughter. I lacked what God has said in his Word to be good (Ps. 127:3). The many happenings concerning my heart recorded in the preceding pages—like it being remade, singing with peace, and releasing sorrow to God—did not erase my wound.

So, how greatly I appreciated that in 2 Corinthians 5:4, the apostle Paul freely acknowledges "groans" and "being burdened" as part of the Christian life! The author of Hebrews further validates that to retain longing is biblical: believers are "strangers" who are "longing for a better country—a heavenly one" (Heb. 11:13b, 16a NIV). A stranger on earth, burdened and groaning, who was watching expectantly for her homeland—that sounded like me.

When I was tempted to love heaven to the exclusion of earth, I learned that expectant hope for heaven fueled my continuing life on earth. I knew that the God who would be with me in the future day of glory was also with me on this earth too. Yet, I ached for her. Because I could determine the longing to have my stillborn daughter near as compatible with Scripture, my question became how to steward well the longing within.

Although eternity will resolve my groaning and long-carried burdens, it is not the only balm for the pains the apostle Paul lists (2 Cor. 5:4–5). As long as my unfulfilled longings exist—and even after the burdens are relieved in eternal rest—Paul's proposed method for stewarding my longings well is to please the Lord (2 Cor. 5:9). That simple instruction is more glorious than a first glance might afford.

In *principle*, God has taught that children are a good gift. Yet, in his *plans*—his trajectory for each life—he has not deemed that all people receive all like good gifts. Biblical and systematic theology professor, John Feinberg, whose wife was diagnosed with an incurable, genetically transmitted disease, writes:

> When philosophers discuss the concept of justice, they distinguish between what is called *distributive justice* and *egalitarian justice*. With distributive justice, each person gets exactly what is deserved. If you do good, in strict justice you are owed

good. If you do evil, in strict justice you deserve punishment. Egalitarian justice, however, gives everyone the same thing, regardless of merit or desert.

Now I saw the source of the problem. It isn't just that sufferers think distributive justice mandates a better fate for them (since they think they have done good). The complaint is that God should operate with egalitarian justice in his handling of the world. We expect him to treat everyone the same, and that means we should escape a specific affliction if others do! Otherwise, it seems that God has been unfair.

Once I remembered the distinction between these two types of justice, I immediately asked why God is obligated to dole out suffering and blessing on the basis of egalitarian justice. Given the demands of distributive justice, all sinners *deserve* nothing but punishment. Why, then, is God obligated to respond to us in egalitarian terms? I couldn't answer that. If God really did handle us according to egalitarian justice, we would all experience the same torture or be equally blessed. But those ideas don't match the God described in Scripture. It was a tremendous help to realize that part of my anger stemmed from thinking that God is obligated to handle us with egalitarian justice, even though he isn't. Once I realized that he has no such obligation, I understood that much of my anger rested on a misunderstanding of what God should be expected to do.[1]

According to Feinberg's view, God determines in his sovereign, wise, and mysterious will, upon whom he will bestow the good gift of children. When the disciple Peter is told by Jesus that he would endure suffering, he looks to John, the beloved disciple, and essentially asks, "What about him? Will he have to endure that suffering?" Jesus' answer is, "What is that to you? You follow me!" (Jn. 21:22b).

I readily concede that a dear, unfilled longing inspires little gratitude. And yet, when that same longing is viewed as a stewardship of suffering borne out of love for the Lord, the load to carry changes altogether.[2] If I can bear my longing for the purpose of loving him, joy accompanies the sorrow, and my heart is lifted. The sorrow remains, but if my sorrow is viewed as being endured for the sake of the Lord, it becomes ennobled by virtue of and association with him! To bear such a loss for the sake of knowing Christ and seeing him glorified all the more—when put like that? The release of a decision to "let" his wise plan proceed without protest becomes wonderfully compelled by him (2 Cor. 5:14).

Some months after my loss, I blogged:

> I will not ask any questions of my Lord in eternity when I come face-to-face with him. So, I do not ask any questions today either. Many think that those who have experienced loss, by necessity, have unresolved questions—questions which we will ask the Lord in eternity. I have none. I will have none before the magnificence of my Lord, upon my first sight of him whom I love—of that I am assured. So, I have none now.
>
> I do look forward with great joy to learning any ways at all he has been glorified through my life—I can think of no greater joy than to know that I have served him. What a thought is that—me serving the Lord—in itself! Is that not a great reward?

I remember my heavy breath of labor, the shape my face made with my first tears upon seeing her, the weight of her body in my arms. I remember how her skin felt to my love-giving lips, the appearance of her open, empty mouth when I first saw her come, how she changed by the hand of death. I remember her lying motionless to be measured and weighted—feeling she was not made to lay lifeless, but to be held as close to life as possible, if not living. I remember giving her body to the nurse and her walking that dear frame out of the door, out of my earthly life.

But in all of those moments, she was already free—she loved him fully in the splendor and truth of the heavenly places. Though in principle, fully experiencing the love of two earthly parents would have been good, it was not a part of God's earthly plan for her. When I consider God's good plan for her from the standpoint of eternity, I do not doubt it, so neither should I ever doubt his plans for me, viewed also from the standpoint of eternity and the immeasurable gain of seeing my Lord and hearing him say, "Well done" (Matt. 25:23).

Since the day her body went devastatingly limp, I have gained more time and capacity for the inner reception of Christ's love. The Lord has used my daughter's life in mine—I have greater love for the Lord and his life through the gift of knowing her. This I know: what could possibly draw any two people closer than the Lord himself—and the shared eternal love of the almighty God, which produces the most life-altering experience of all? *Nothing.*

Would having my daughter with me be a wonderful, good gift? I can only imagine so, yes. But yet, is there a better way God might be served? By his sovereign hand in my life, I have concluded that for the present, yes. I am not him, with an infinitely wise mind weaving together a quantity of realities I cannot enumerate. In the present, I know this: I only want my longings to be fulfilled if they serve him—from his hand, for his sake. If this present reality is what most serves him, despite my mourning and groans, what I most desire is a heart set on him, beating for the Lord Jesus, "releasing" myself and my daughter to the service of divine aims.

Not many weeks after my loss, I remember talking with my mom about a new brand of food I had enthusiastically discovered: the "Enjoy Life" brand, especially wonderful for those with food intolerances. I could eat chocolate—a proximate comfort, indeed—worry-free. My dad came in partway through the conversation, and my mom and I noted his somewhat somber tone, nodding and sighing with us in agreement in the corner of the room. I appreciated the new chocolate but did not realize my dad appreciated my ability to eat chocolate to this extent.

My mom, noticing the same, asked, "What do you think we're talking about?"

"Lianna making it a point to enjoy life again?" he replied.

We laughed. But the point was not lost on me—part of worship is receiving the happiness that God does decide to give, even after one longed-for happiness is not given.

PRAYER OF HOPE

Father,

Guide me now with your ever-loving hand. One day, lead me home to that place longed-for through the ages, the eternal land. There, please, may it be said of me that I lived and served for the sake of you, the only Person who could make my heart of stone new.

To know my child, I ache; she is your joyous gift. But I know that she is eternally happy and blessed in the place of no tears, where nothing is even slightly amiss; I also grasp now that my own happiness in whatever you choose for my life is no dismissal of your gift of her. Instead, part of worship is to gratefully and humbly receive everything good, joyous, and even happy, that you do have plans to give.

Receiving and partaking of your rich blessings, how sweet to think I share this with the baby I have seen, but never met. Thank you that I can most think of closeness with her not in the torrents of earthly sadness, but in the depths of your eternally shared love. To you alone, my God, my worship I lift.

Thank you for making my heart of stone into flesh and for showing me that because of Christ's sacrifice and glory I changelessly stand as one who is graciously blessed. I love you, Lord.

In the name of Jesus,
Amen

ONE DAY IN GLORY

Lindsey Dennis

And a voice came from the throne, saying,
"Give praise to our God, all you His bond-servants, you who
fear Him, the small and the great."
Then I heard something like the voice of a great multitude
and like the sound of many waters and like
the sound of mighty peals of thunder, saying,
"Hallelujah! For the Lord our God, the Almighty, reigns."
—Revelation 19:5–6 NASB

I can only imagine the sound John heard—the sound he could only describe as "something like" a great multitude, "something like" the sound of many waters, "something like" the sound of mighty peals of thunder. Something so loud, so wondrous, so awesome, so astounding that the only way he could describe what he heard was through mere attempts at comparison with his own experience.

And yet, because what he heard was both like and unlike anything he had ever heard before, he hardly knew how to compare it.

I live in Florida, where thunderstorms are a daily summer experience. I am used to the thunder and the rain and have always enjoyed a good thunderstorm. Yet one day, a thunderstorm passed that seemed as though it was on top of our house. I saw lightning seemingly strike the house next door (it did not) and heard thunder so loud that I braced myself every time I saw light flash out of the corner of my eye. A split second later, the house shook. It was both terrifying and awe-inspiring. It was the sound of a battle raging all around.

In my church, we sing songs of "hallelujah!" with various tempos and beats, some soft and introspective, others loud and joyful. The words John writes in Revelation will be heard in the context of a holy victory and celebration. They are the response to a battle won, ending in righteousness, justice, and in life for God's people. It will not be a soft, introspective cry. It will be loud, thunderous, and filled with the kind of emotions that come when victory is decidedly won, once and for all. And this glorious "hallelujah!" will come from the multitude of bond-servants: the multitude of men and women who have followed Christ, whose names are written in the book of life, whose lives bear the mark of Jesus—and I have the hope that it includes our babies who have gone before us.

One comparison for what this moment might be like comes from when I have been at a professional football game. My team appears to be losing but comes from behind, and in a stunning play, takes the lead at the last possible second to win the game. And what happens? The crowd goes wild. You hug and high-five everyone who is cheering for your team too—stranger or friend, grinning from ear to ear toward them all. It is celebration, and it is victory. That example is nothing, I know, in comparison to the moment God's people will all shout "hallelujah!" together.

Often when I stand in church for worship, and we are singing a song that testifies to the greatness of God or points to the day when we will be with him forever, I hold my hands out on either side. I imagine moments after the establishment of the new heaven and the new earth, when I am worshipping the Lamb who was slain for me, for all believers, and for my two daughters now with Jesus. I imagine holding my hands out to either side, my daughters' hands filling mine. And I think about what it will be like to worship the King and to sing "hallelujah!" with them by my side. I imagine pulling them near and having joy no longer tainted by sadness, saying, "The battle is over, death and sin are defeated, all of his promises have been fulfilled, and *all* has been made new! Worthy is the Lamb who was slain, worthy is the King! Great is your name!"

The joy of worshipping our King in glory will, I know, be far greater than I could even imagine, but this future is highlighted in my heart because of the pain of losing my first two daughters. When I was twenty weeks pregnant with my first daughter, Sophie, we found out that she had a condition that would not allow her to live once born. We chose to celebrate her life, carrying her to term and welcoming her into our arms for ten precious hours of breath. Then, in a shocking blow to our already deeply grieving hearts, we found out nine months later that the second child I was carrying, another daughter, also had a similar condition. Again, we celebrated her life, carried her to term, and welcomed our second daughter, Dasah, into the world, delighting in all twelve hours of breath God gave her.

I do not understand why God has allowed such pain and loss to be written into our story. God has done much to restore our broken hearts and bring purpose from our pain in the years since the loss of our girls, but I still miss and deeply long for them and wonder why they could not stay. Paul writes in 1 Corinthians 13:12 NIV, "For now we see only a reflection as in a mirror; then we shall see face to face. Now I know in part; then I shall know fully, even as I am fully known." Just as I imagine the joy of utter praise and worship for the King, I also imagine the moment I will look into the face of Jesus. Perhaps my girls will be by my side, and I will see a tender smile erupt from his face as he looks at me, knowing that I now fully understand—as far as God will make my humanly mind able—the reason for this pain. That moment when I see in full, with complete resolution, what I only knew in part this side of heaven.

I do not know whether I will stand before the King and shout victory cries with my first two daughters—and other family members who have believed—by my side. I imagine that when I see him face-to-face, I will be far more focused on Christ than who is by my side. All hearts of the people there will be united and so full because of Christ alone. But for now, these glimpses of glory lift my eyes to the joy that is coming—the hope that will be fulfilled and the brokenness all made new. What I do know is when that day comes, I will fully know, I will fully worship, and I will shout the victory cry, a glorious "hallelujah!" for the King who has defeated sin and death and their effects once and for all.

And I will see all that I could not see in this life, all that I could not make sense of and could only describe, like John, as "it will be 'something like' this." I wonder in the midst of the chapters in my story that feel so broken and full of pain, what invisible-to-me pages exist between the broken ones. What story is God penning for all of creation, for my little life to experience while woven into the greater plan for his glory to go forth in all the earth? One day in heaven, I will know.

I will shout "hallelujah!" without doubt, without fear, and without grief. Every theme of brokenness in the stories of God's people will find newness. Tears will be wiped away and replaced with a joy unimaginable, a glory unbelievable, and most of all, the Savior incomparable. One day in heaven.

> And I heard a loud voice from the throne, saying, "Behold, the tabernacle of God is among men, and He will dwell among them, and they shall be His people, and God Himself will be among them, and He will wipe away every tear from their eyes; and there will no longer be any death; there will no longer be any mourning, or crying, or pain; the first things have passed away." And He who sits on the throne said, "Behold, I am making all things new." And He said, "Write, for these words are faithful and true."
> —Revelation 21:3–5 NASB

PRAYER OF HOPE

Hallelujah! For you, my Lord, reign! Today I cannot grasp the fullness of what it will be like to stand before you and cry out in praise and worship and adoration without the grief that often hovers over me. But I praise you in faith and in hope as I look to that day when you will make all things new. The day when I will stand before you and more fully understand the story you were writing for my life, for my children's lives and for all of creation. I praise you today that you are the one who will defeat death once and for all, and you are the one who makes all things new. I may not understand my story now, but I look in hope to the day when I will, and I choose to honor and glorify and worship your holy name in faith as I sit in the kingdom that has come and long for the kingdom coming. Jesus you are wonderful, you are glorious, you are King, and you are victorious. And I join with all the saints who groan today in eager anticipation for the redemption of all things: "Maranatha. Come, Lord Jesus. Come quickly."

Amen

He Has Been Found

Moving forward on solid ground

When our grief was still recent, Tyler and I reclined at a Lake Michigan beach. We breathed chilly air, looking at the vast blue— the closest we could come to an ocean living in the Midwest. I mused about themes of eternity in that endlessness. We swatted at a few pesky flies, mostly in solitude together except for a few passersby in the distance whose frames eventually faded into a long stretch of sand. For me, this subtle act felt bold. It was one of my first attempts to return to the "real" world.[1]

I never would have been at the beach that day had my daughter been on earth. Every day I could not be in heaven, my heart spoke themes of eternity to me. The cool air turned into a chill through my body. I wished I had brought a coat. More, the now-swarming flies threatened to diminish my little attempt at boldness; they won back their territory. My arms were tired of flailing after only a few uncomfortable minutes.

Settling into the car for another forty-minute drive, I tried to brush away our little beach experience as an anomaly in an otherwise precious period of time. We felt love pouring upon us from other people after our daughter fell asleep, and I knew God's steady presence as I gave birth and accomplished different tasks related to her funeral. Yet, part of returning to the "real" world was to know that activities would not continue to feel so momentous. The grandly generous gestures of others, the sweeping thoughts of eternity, and the new and extensive understanding of death—which magnified Christ's ability to crush it—would not be maintained at the same level of intensity of experience. Some days simply involved swatting flies away and shuffling through the sand back to the car from a cold beach trip that ended too soon. It was not an anomaly; it was part of the rest of my life. And living the rest of my life on this earth seemed beyond my comprehension. I wanted to brush the whole of it aside as unimportant, as not what really mattered compared with the latest days consumed with sacred thoughts or the future days of heavenly realities.

But the pesky days of earthly life returned to me—even when brushed away. And I could not ultimately retreat from them. I had to relearn to live them.

What in grief is passing, even if slowly passing; what is becoming habitual? What is symptomatic of the cloud of grief, and what arises from attitudes of the heart? These are the kinds of questions I have learned to ask of my grief.

I wonderfully retreated many times from normal life—as suits my disposition—communing with God, releasing my tears, and examining the various facets of my grief in order to understand it as I do now. I did not retreat due to a jaded disposition in my heart;

I knew that I would keep taking steps forward after that early Lake Michigan trip. But to take time for privacy was fitting—after all, how much time King David must have spent in quiet repose composing the eloquent psalms from which I was dearly benefitting! I knew those quiet hours of tears and truth-seeking to be good and necessary because my relationship with God was foremost to me, and I had work to do with him. Simultaneously, I also knew the extended solitude to be part of the passing cloud—not a new, defining trajectory for how I would come to live.

I once wondered what purpose God could have in the moments of silent tears no one saw, but in hindsight, those times produced the clearing for a fluidity of thought about the truths of the Lord that could not otherwise have been afforded—holy messages essential for me that were made ready for expression to others through retreat. I think of King David as an example, who used his moments of quiet pain, tears, and truth-seeking to write the book of Psalms, the songbook of Israel.

Just as my cloud of grief brought with it a need for extended times of quiet repose, the cloud of grief also affected my experience of God. I had difficulty remembering God's goodness. I acknowledged that to him. This difficulty was a symptom of grief's storm clouds, dense with threatening, navy rage as they hovered around me. As with retreating, this was not due to a negative disposition of my heart. I did not revolt against God's goodness; I did not experience disdain that words of his goodness were recorded in Scripture for me to read. I did not think God owed me answers or owed me anything. I simply could not see him very well at all. So, when I wrote of his goodness, I caused myself to remember.

Lacking recollection of the goodness of God was not evidence of a freshly forming theological ground; no, the clouds were passing.[2] For I was already set, by his grace, on a strong theological foundation, one to which my feet could return—and, certainly, a foundation that could be first found *after* grief as well.

The beach we boldly visited, though chilly, was still attracting some people who were living their everyday lives; these quickly disappearing frames were faint echoes of "real" life in the world around me, that I would grow into again, in some old ways and some new ways. Similarly, when I was primarily thinking about my daughter, there were echoes of larger spiritual realities beyond me and my needs, evidencing a good God who cannot change. This grander view of God's unalterable goodness was the foundation to which I returned, and upon which I grew.

It had once seemed natural, even right, that the world outside of my personal grief felt strange to me. But in order to relearn my steps, I would keep revisiting the outside world, traveling around a part of the spiral to new grounds. Similarly, to relearn my spiritual life on new ground meant seeing myself again as integrated into God's plan—with him as the center of my life.

Knowing him near, I poured my heart's tears into the infinite reservoir of my sovereign Lord; but knowing him to be holy, I still needed to watch my steps before the throne of a God whose plans are beyond me and my life (Eccl. 5:1). And though I received, with thanks, his gracious provisions of orchestrating my minutes and showing love to me through others, he was deserving of being worshipped and cherished regardless of those provisions. D. Martyn Lloyd-Jones writes,

> We must always be careful to emphasise that the knowledge of God comes before any particular blessing that we may desire from Him. The goal of all our seeking and all our worship and all our endeavour should not be to have a particular experience; it should not be to petition certain blessings; it should be to

know God Himself—the Giver not the gift, the source and the fount of every blessing, not the blessing itself.

I think you will agree with me that we always need that reminder. We are all of us so prone to start with ourselves and our problems. Sometimes I am almost filled with alarm as I get the impression from certain people and books that really they are not interested in God at all except as an agency who can give them blessings, for that is surely wrong and utterly unbiblical. Listen to our Lord Himself saying it: 'Blessed are the pure in heart: for they shall see God'—that is the *summum bonum*; that is our end and object and goal.[3]

To know God—that I could, that I do!

I knew death's status with me: an enemy that Christ had defeated whose completed destruction is still to come (1 Cor. 15:26). But I also saw that, before God, death is just. Though death is a despised enemy that will not be part of his all-things-new eternity, it is scriptural to affirm that God is good to have inflicted mankind with death—he said he would if his directive was disregarded (Gen. 2:17), and when sorrowfully required, he surely did. And through this, I know that he can be trusted to keep his word and be righteous and good always—even knowing the scorn he would receive throughout the ages for this righteousness from those he was being gracious to allow to still live!

I am brought temporary anguish—for that is what this grief is, *temporary*—because of sin and the just consequences of sin. But without his righteous rule, what hope could I have for eternity? Without his righteous, uncompromising authority, I would weep continuously—as the apostle John was beginning to do in the dramatic unfolding of prophecy in Revelation 5:1–4—because otherwise no one worthy to make all things right could be found.

Then I saw in the right hand of him who was seated on the throne a scroll written within and on the back, sealed with seven seals. And I saw a mighty angel proclaiming with a loud voice, "Who is worthy to open the scroll and break its seals?" And no one in heaven or on earth or under the earth was able to open the scroll or to look into it, and I began to weep loudly because no one was found worthy to open the scroll to look into it.

Biblical expositor James M. Hamilton Jr. notes that the writing on the scrolls "relates to the events that will bring history to its appointed conclusion."[4] Why did John mourn when these scrolls were unopened?

If the scroll were not opened,

- [Revelation] 5:9, Jesus would not be worshiped as worthy to open the scroll.
- 5:9, Jesus would not be worshiped as the world's Redeemer.
- 6:10, the martyrs of the faith would not be avenged.
- 8:4, 5, the prayers of the saints ("Your will be done; your kingdom come") would not be answered.
- 9:15, God's appointed plan would not come to pass.
- 11:15, the kingdom of the world would not become the kingdom of our Lord and of his Christ.
- 16–18, the wicked would not be judged.
- 19, 20, Jesus would not come back.
- 21, 22, God would not reign in glory in the new heavens and the new earth.

In short, if that scroll isn't opened, the Bible's promises don't come true. Hope is defeated.[5]

But the apostle John continues in verse 5, "And one of the elders said to me, 'Weep no more; behold, the Lion of the tribe of Judah, the Root of David, has conquered, so that he can open the scroll and its seven seals.'"

He has been found.

In the early, unfolding scenes of Genesis, mankind was created at the Lord's command (Gen. 1:26), and mankind was made to flourish through obedience to his commands (Gen. 1:28–31, 2:15–17). And now, I know him, the one who fulfilled while in the flesh every command (Matt. 5:17–18) when I could not. He is mine by faith, and he is worthy to execute all of his just, righteous, good, and very precious plans. As I wait for his coming, I see through these early chapters in Genesis this principle for life on solid ground: wherever his righteous rule is well received, there dwells his perfect peace (Isa. 26:3; Ps. 119:143).

I have hope I will see my daughter again. She is my dear. I am proud to be her mom. I miss her soul. I miss her presence in my life. I felt like I knew her. I feel like I do. I still wish we were together—this will never feel "right." She is my girl, and I love her. I am grateful to have known her. It was "too short." I have all of my memories of her stored as treasures. A favorite is the first blanket that the hospital wrapped around her little frame because I can still touch an item that touched her. And I adore when people reference her as a real part of our family (because she is). There are times when I cannot explain how greatly I yearn for the pace of this life to go into overdrive. Every holiday and birthday is one gratefully had here—but also is one closer to eternal, overcoming glory.

And with all I feel for her and much more than can hardly be written, I know that I cannot live for her. I cannot get up every day and face the continuing days of "real" life because of her memory. She is so beloved. But there is only one God. Only he could have been to me through this grief who God has been. He has been my infinite, patient, purpose-giving, gentle, holy Shepherd.

Throughout my early grief, I often went to bed without reading a single new verse of Scripture that day. At various points along my grief, I felt a truth land so heavily upon me that I could not possibly read anything new for a while. It took days to decompress.

For all of those nights I could not retain anything new, I went back to a well-worn passage now so familiar without becoming remotely shallow-sounding for all of its use. Head on my pillow, I would remember these words, and sleep beneath the canopy of their truth.

Psalm 23

The LORD is my shepherd; I shall not want.

He gives me peace with turning my desires over to whatever purposes will ultimately fulfill his good pleasure.

He makes me lie down in green pastures.
He leads me beside still waters.

He stores all of my tears in his bottle, recording my grief (Ps. 56:8).

He restores my soul.

He shows me that being restored to life would not dismiss any love for my daughter— but that I can love her best in him who is eternal.

He leads me in paths of righteousness for his name's sake.

He enables me to believe that no evil comes from his hand.

Even though I walk through the valley of the shadow of death, I will fear no evil, for you are with me;

> *Though I thought I would die in the hospital room or enter a purposeless pit as a mother with no child to mother, living for him has rescued me. Because I have his presence and breath, I also have purpose.*

Your rod and your staff, they comfort me.

> *He teaches me to remember that to be true and faithful to him would never conflict with my desire to be true to myself and faithful to my daughter.*

You prepare a table before me in the presence of my enemies; you anoint my head with oil; my cup overflows.

> *He assures me that no passing comment from the breath of human lips will overcome his design. My daughter's life has meaning because he created her; no one can take that away.*

Surely goodness and mercy shall follow me all the days of my life,

> *He restores my feet to good ground. He clears my storm clouds. He mercifully enables me to walk forward again.*

and I shall dwell in the house of the Lord forever.

> *He gives me an eternal hope.*

Through the witness of my beloved daughter in my life and the eternal promises of Scripture, I have felt and believed that what is ahead is weightier and more real. For through this experience—this refining by fire—I am connected to the beautiful light of heaven. Like strands of a tapestry, otherworldly gold is woven securely, solidly into me. I have a sure hope that goes around the corner of this world to glory, or in the words of Scripture, "a sure and steadfast anchor of the soul, a hope that enters into the inner places behind the curtain" (Heb. 6:19). My soul is connected through Christ to the better, glorious place just behind the curtain of this world. God has made my daughter for a different land; he has made me for a different land too.

Nothing that I have done (or will do) fills the gap between me and my daughter or me and my Lord—no writing, no ministry, no love, no change of heart, no sense or emotion, no good work. Rather, he planned from the beginning of time to send his Son to die for my sins (1 Pet. 1:20; Acts 2:23) that I might treasure him and know him to be faithful all of my days—he who keeps his Word. Early church father John Chrysostom taught, "This gives those who hear it full assurance; it relieves them to be told, that whatever He promises, for His own goodness' sake He will most surely perform."[6] The basis of my hope—the foundation for continuing day-to-day life—is this: he will always be true to all that he has said and all of who he is.

Of my life's loving obedience, he is worthy. My purpose and the one dearest to me? *He has been found.*

ACKNOWLEDGMENTS

My first expression of gratitude belongs to my husband, Tyler, a supportive, stabling force who long carried the weight of our lives so that I could write—and did so with a joyful willingness that would never mention such a contribution. Doing my thinking while having your trustworthy and charitable maturity in Christ as part of my day-to-day environment has lifted me from the pressures of conformity for the sake of conformity. In this, you have allowed me to experience greater freedom to serve the Lord as the person he created me to be. In suffering, grief, and life, you I admire most.

My second daughter I did not know when I wrote most of these words. But all along the way, God was preparing me not only for returning to earthly life again—more specifically, he was also readying me for you, sweetheart. Imagine! And he has continued to restore my life through simple truths you have spoken to me and through observing the exuberant joy you can experience, even in a fallen world. You are right—it is also a beautiful world. My heart is all yours too, my girl—and has been every step of the way.

Undoubtedly my parents, Martin and Sheryl Kroeker, are the unattributed voices behind a countless number of this book's thoughts. You have spoken to me and Tyler much of what has been most understanding, truth-filled, and meaningful after loss. We grieved together, and you were rocks for me. In addition to teaching me the gospel and embodying godly devotion to the Lord, helping to instill in me a love for Scripture from an early age is the best gift you have given me. I am indebted.

To my husband, parents, grandparents, siblings, siblings-in-law, and parents-in-law who were also anticipating a treasured baby and grieved—I am grateful for every memory.

My maternal grandfather, David J. Hesselgrave—now with the Lord—used his gifts of writing, knowledge, generous love, and wisdom for our good. For example, the open letter he wrote to Noelle (see the prologue of this book) held some of the first words I read after our loss, directing my thoughts. The devotionals he sent for many days following, at my request, kept me solidly in Scripture when I could hardly think of where in it to turn. In short, when I think of whom I want to emulate, aside from the obvious, it is him.

LifeSpring Community Church, you felt our loss with us and were like family to us. Your love I will not forget.

Pastor Colin Smith, Dr. Pam MacRae, Erin Cushman, Dave DeWit, Josh and Bethany Dennis, Hannah Lannigan, Beth Barthelemy, and Lorelei Gauger all imparted courage to me in various ways when the writing was just beginning some years ago. In part, I kept pursuing this work because of you all.

This project could not have moved forward as it did without the generosity of Abigail Priebe, Katie Swider, and Meredith Hodge. You helped me and Hope Mommies from your hearts for God's glory.

Brittnie Blackburn, Stephanie Blanks, Lindsey Dennis, Abigail Eades, Sam Martin, Ashlee Schmidt, Meg Walker, and Calli Williams, when I first started writing these words, I did not know you—and could not have had you in mind. How grateful I am that God did! Your sisterhood amidst loss and grief is a precious part of my life.

Constance Ray and Julie Karen Hodgins, thank you for extending your gifts of polished design to this project, bringing it to completion.

Carla Vick of Hope Mommies, your uplifting feedback on the manuscript was bolstering. Hope Mommies leadership team and board, your support of this project is cherished.

Jennifer Parks of Hope Mommies, thank you for championing this book, for your wisdom throughout the months toward publication, and for your leadership that is characterized by selflessness. I likely would not have met you apart from our mutual connection with Hope Mommies. So all the more, I am eternally grateful for your true partnership in the gospel.

Notes

Chapter One

1.   Kevin Zuber was my college systematic theology professor at
     Moody Bible Institute.

Chapter Two

1.   John Piper, "Why Do You Believe That Infants
     Who Die Go to Heaven?" Desiring God, January
     30, 2008, https://www.desiringgod.org/interviews/
     why-do-you-believe-that-infants-who-die-go-to-heaven.

2.   MacArthur, John F., *Safe in the Arms of God: Truth from Heaven
     About the Death of a Child* (Nashville: Thomas Nelson, 2003), 80
     (italics in the original).

3.   R. Albert Mohler Jr. and Daniel L. Akin, "The Salvation
     of the 'Little Ones': Do Infants Who Die Go to Heaven?"
     AlbertMohler.com, July 16, 2009, http://www.albertmohler.
     com/2009/07/16/the-salvation-of-the-little-ones-do-infants-
     who-die-go-to-heaven/ (emphasis mine).

4. B. B. Warfield, *The Development of the Doctrine of Infant Salvation* (Shawnee, KS: Primedia eLaunch, 2011), Kindle edition, Kindle location 503–504.

5. Ibid., Kindle location 511–512.

6 Ibid., Kindle location 511–512.

7. Ibid., Kindle location 515–517.

8. Charles H. Spurgeon, "Expositions of the Doctrines of Grace," *Metropolitan Tabernacle Pulpit*, vol. 7 (London: Passmore and Alabaster, 1862), 300, quoted in John F. MacArthur, *Safe in the Arms of God: Truth from Heaven About the Death of a Child* (Nashville: Thomas Nelson, 2003), 75 (emphasis mine).

9. James M. Freeman and Harold J. Chadwick, "Benedictions on Children" in *Manners & Customs of the Bible* (North Brunswick, NJ: Bridge-Logos Publishers, 1998), 445.

CHAPTER THREE

1. John Piper, "For Noel On Our 25th Wedding Anniversary," Desiring God, December 19, 1993, https://www.desiringgod.org/articles/for-noel-on-our-25th-wedding-anniversary.

2. C. S. Lewis, *The Problem of Pain* (1940; reprint, New York: HarperOne, 2001), 91. Citations refer to the 2001 edition.

3. John Donne, "Death, Be Not Proud," Poetry Foundation, accessed September 24, 2018, https://www.poetryfoundation.org/poems/44107/holy-sonnets-death-be-not-proud.

4. Jonathan Edwards, *The Works of President Edwards* (New York: Leavitt & Allen, 1851), 537, https://books.google.com/books?id=3u_WAAAAMAAJ&source=gbs_navlinks_s.

5. D. A. Carson, *How Long, O Lord?: Reflections of Suffering and Evil*, 2nd edition (Grand Rapids: Baker Academic, 2006), 44.

6. I imagine that the particular manifestations of his grace vary for every person. I share my experience not because I consider

it to be remarkably different from others', but because it is the testimony I have and know.

CHAPTER FOUR

1. Thomas Ken, "Praise God from Whom All Blessings Flow," Hymnary.org, Accessed October 9, 2018, https://hymnary.org/text/praise_god_from_whom_all_blessings_ken.

2. C. S. Lewis, *Mere Christianity* (Reprint, New York: HarperOne, 2002) 25, quoted in Nancy Guthrie, *The One Year Book of Hope* (Detroit: Christian Large Print, 2012), epigraph.

3. Charles H. Dyer, "Jeremiah," in *The Bible Knowledge Commentary: An Exposition of the Scriptures*, eds. J. F. Walvoord and R. B. Zuck (Wheaton: Victor Books, 1985), 1:1149.

4. Emphasis mine.

CHAPTER FIVE

1. Emphasis mine.

2. I do not mean to indicate a belief that my daughter is still a baby in heaven.

CHAPTER SIX

1. This and the preceding four quotations are from George Matheson, "O Love That Wilt Not Let Me Go," hymnary.org, accessed October 9, 2018, https://hymnary.org/text/o_love_that_wilt_not_let_me_go.

CHAPTER SEVEN

1. Scripture teaches the believer's entrance into heaven is not given because of his or her good works—no merely good human works could possibly merit heaven. A believer is welcomed there solely based upon the merit of Jesus Christ being given, or credited, to the believer by grace through faith—a grateful faith that enables

good works to spring forth with joy. So, without any intentions of confusing the scriptural clarity of that doctrine for the reader, I include Lewis' dramatic sketch here.

2. C. S. Lewis, *The Great Divorce* (1946; repr., New York: HarperOne, 2001), 97; ibid., 98–99. Citations refer to the 2001 edition.

3. Ibid.

4. Luke 11:27–28 NIV reads, "As Jesus was saying these things, a woman in the crowd called out, 'Blessed is the mother who gave you birth and nursed you.' He replied, 'Blessed rather are those who hear the word of God and obey it.'"

Chapter Eight

1. George Herbert, "Grief," *The Complete English Poems* (New York: Penguin Books, 2004), 154.

Chapter Nine

1. Charles H. Spurgeon, "The Third Beatitude," *Spurgeon's Sermons Volume 53: 1907* (Grand Rapids: Christian Classics Ethereal Library, n.d.), accessed September 11, 2018, www.ccel.org/ccel/spurgeon/sermons53.xlv.html, quoted in Colin Smith, "Cultivating Meekness," Unlocking the Bible, October 24, 2012, www.unlockingthebible.org/sermon/cultivating-meekness.

2. This point from my pastor, Colin Smith's, sermon entitled "Cultivating Meekness" has remained with me. Colin Smith, "Cultivating Meekness," Unlocking the Bible, October 24, 2012, www.unlockingthebible.org/sermon/cultivating-meekness.

Chapter Eleven

1. S. Lewis Johnson, *Discovering Romans: Spiritual Revival for the Soul* (Grand Rapids: Zondervan, 2014), 136.

2. Martyn Lloyd-Jones, *Great Doctrines of the Bible, Volume 1: God the Father, God the Son* (Wheaton: Crossway, 1996), 66–67.

CHAPTER TWELVE

1. Colin Smith, "Tears and Talk," Unlocking the Bible, April 3, 2017, www.unlockingthebible.org/sermon/tears-talk.

2. Later, after writing these words, I found this quote in C. S. Lewis' *A Grief Observed*—grateful I had come to see an answer: "For in grief nothing 'stays put.' One keeps on emerging from a phase, but it always recurs. Round and round. Everything repeats. Am I going in circles, or dare I hope I am on a spiral? But if a spiral, am I going up or down it?" C. S. Lewis, *A Grief Observed*. (1961; repr., New York: HarperOne, 1996), 56–57. Citations refer to the 1996 edition.

CHAPTER THIRTEEN

1. Matthew Henry, *Matthew Henry's Commentary on the Whole Bible*, vol. VI, Acts to Revelation (Peabody, Massachusetts: Hendrickson Publishers, 1991, second printing 1992) 951, (italics in the original).

CHAPTER FOURTEEN

1. Lactantius, *De Ira Dei*, 51, quoted in Walter C. Kaiser Jr., *A Biblical Approach to Personal Suffering* (Chicago: Moody Press, 1982), 61.

2. C. S. Lewis, *The Problem of Pain* (1940; repr., New York: HarperOne, 2001), 91. Citations refer to the 2001 edition.

CHAPTER FIFTEEN

1. John Feinberg, *Where is God?: A Personal Story of Finding God in Grief and Suffering* (Nashville: Broadman & Holman Publishers, 2004), 73–74 (italics in the original).

2. Marty Kroeker, "Q: Why Me? Why Do I Have to Go Through This?" Hope Mommies, October 9, 2017, https://hopemommies.org/q-why-me-why-do-i-have-to-go-through-this.

EPILOGUE

1. To me, it was the less real world; I am referring to the world that keeps going after shocking loss happens.
2. What told me this was self-examination of my heart.
3. Martyn Lloyd-Jones, *Great Doctrines of the Bible (Three Volumes in One): God the Father, God the Son; God the Holy Spirit; The Church and the Last Things* (Wheaton: Crossway, 2003), 50.
4. James M. Hamilton Jr., *Revelation: The Spirit Speaks to the Churches*, Preaching the Word, ed. R. Kent Hughes (Wheaton: Crossway, 2012), 152.
5. Ibid., 153.
6. John Chrysostom, *Saint Chrysostom: Homilies on Galatians, Ephesians, Philippians, Colossians, Thessalonians, Timothy, Titus, and Philemon*, Nicene and Post-Nicene Fathers Series I, Vol. 13, ed. Philip Schaff (Grand Rapids: Christian Classics Ethereal Library, n.d.), 110, http://www.ccel.org/s/schaff/npnf113/cache/npnf113.pdf.

BIBLIOGRAPHY

Carson, D. A. 2006. *How Long, O Lord?: Reflections of Suffering and Evil.* 2nd. Grand Rapids: Baker Academic.

Dyer, Charles H. 1985. *Jeremiah.* Vol. 1, edited by J. F. Walvoord and R. B. Zuck, 1149. Wheaton: Victor Books.

Feinberg, John. 2004. *Where is God?: A Personal Story of Finding God in Grief and Suffering.* Nashville: Broadman & Holman Publishers.

Freeman, James F., and Harold J. Chadwick. 1998. "Benedictions on Children." In *Manners & Customs of the Bible.* North Brunswick: Bridge-Logos Publishers.

Hughes, R. Kent. n.d. *The Lamb Standing as Though Slain.* Accessed September 23, 2018. https://www. esv.org/resources/preaching-the-word-revelation/ article-the-lamb-standing-as-though-slain/.

Johnson, S. Lewis. 2014. *Discovering Romans: Spiritual Revival for the Soul.* Grand Rapids: Zondervan.

Kaiser Jr., Walter C. 1982. *A Biblical Approach to Personal Suffering.* Chicago: Moody Press.

Ken, Thomas. 1674. *Praise God From Whom All Blessings Flow.* Accessed October 7, 2018. https://hymnary.org/text/praise_god_from_whom_all_blessings_ken.

Lewis, C. S. 1996. *A Grief Observed.* New York: HarperOne.

—. 2001. *The Great Divorce.* New York: HarperSanFrancisco.

—. 2001. *The Problem of Pain.* San Francisco: HarperSan Francisco.

Lloyd-Jones, Martyn. 2012. *Great Doctrines of the Bible (Three Volumes in One): God the Father, God the Son; God the Holy Spirit; The Church and the Last Things.* Wheaton: Crossway.

—. 1996. *Great Doctrines of the Bible, Volume 1: God the Father, God the Son.* Wheaton: Crossway.

MacArthur, John F. 2003. *Safe in the Arms of God: Truth from Heaven About the Death of a Child.* Nashville: Thomas Nelson.

Matheson, George. 1882. *O Love That Wilt Not Let Me Go.* Accessed October 7, 2018. https://hymnary.org/text/o_love_that_wilt_not_let_me_go.

Mohler, R. Albert, and Daniel L. Akin. 2009. *The Salvation of the "Little Ones": Do Infants Who Die Go to Heaven?* July 16. Accessed October 3, 2017. www.albertmohler.com/2009/07/16/the-salvation-of-the-little-ones-do-infants-who-die-go-to-heaven.

Pink, Arthur W. 2008. *The Sovereignty of God.* Blacksburg: Wilder.

Piper, John. 2006. *What Happens to Infants Who Die?* January 23. Accessed April 3, 2017. www.desiringgod.org/articles/what-happens-to-infants-who-die.

Smith, Colin. 2012. *Cultivating Meekness.* October 24. Accessed September 11, 2018. www.unlockingthebible.org/sermon/cultivating-meekness.

—. 2017. *Tears and Talk.* April 3. Accessed September 29, 2018. www.unlockingthebible.org/sermon/tears-talk.

Spurgeon, Charles H. 1873. *The Third Beatitude.* December 11. Accessed September 11, 2018. www.ccel.org/ccel/spurgeon/sermons53.xlv.html.

Warfield, B. B. 2011. *The Development of the Doctrine of Infant Salvation.* Kindle edition. Prod. Primedia eLaunch. Shawnee, Kansas: Primedia eLaunch.

ABOUT THE AUTHOR

Lianna Davis has served in various content and editorial roles with Hope Mommies for the past five years. She also serves as a contributing writer at Unlocking the Bible and is a graduate of Moody Bible Institute with a degree in ministry to women. The suburbs of Chicago are home for her, her husband, and her youngest daughter. She has the great hope that her oldest daughter has gone ahead to be with Christ. More of her writing can be found at liannabdavis.com.

About Hope Mommies

Hope Mommies is a 501(c)3 non-profit organization sharing the hope of Christ with women who have experienced miscarriage, stillbirth, and infant loss. You can connect with Hope Mommies through their annual retreat, online and in-person Bible study groups (Hope Groups), hospital box ministry (Hope Boxes), blog, publications, and more. In their writing and publications, they seek to support the local church by providing biblical resources for baby loss. More information can be found at hopemommies.org. Hope Mommies is on Instagram, Twitter, and Facebook @HopeMommies.

LIST OF CONTRIBUTORS

Brittnie Blackburn lives in Sugar Land, Texas, and enjoys coffee dates, writing on her blog, and soaking in moments with her family. She has two daughters on earth and two babies in heaven, Baby A and Chance Michael. Brittnie is a blog contributor for Hope Mommies, the author of *Desert Song*, and a co-admin for Loved Baby: an online Christian support group for women struggling though miscarriage.

Stephanie Blanks is a Hope Mom to Kinley and lives in Hondo, Texas, with her husband, Matt, and their three other children: Lyston, Levi, and Leighton. She enjoys going to the lake with her family, traveling with her husband, and singing in her church praise band.

Lindsey Dennis lives in Orlando, Florida, with her stud of a husband, Kevin. She has four beautiful children: two with Jesus and two in her arms today. She is the author of *Buried Dreams: From Devastating Loss to Unimaginable Hope*. You can find more of her writing on her personal blog at vaporandmist.com. You can also find her on Instagram @lindseydennis_.

Abigail Eades and her husband, Chad, live on a small family farm in central Kentucky and are parents to two girls: Savannah on earth and Sarabeth who lives with Jesus. In addition to being a stay-at-home mom and teaching piano part-time, Abigail blogs on Facebook @gratitudehealsaheart and Instagram @ahealinggratitude, where her desire is to share Sarabeth's story in a way that highlights the goodness and love of God and how gratitude can lead to greater healing.

Sam Martin is a wife, mother, and work-from-home graphic designer and writer who finds joy in the ordinary. She and her husband, Spencer, have three sons, two with Jesus—Max and "The Martian"—and one in their arms, Lachlan. In addition to working and raising Lachlan, she currently serves on the Board of Directors for the Down Syndrome Guild of Dallas in memory of Max.

Ashlee Schmidt is the Editorial Coordinator for Hope Mommies and author of *I AM* (Hope Mommies, 2016) and *Identity* (Hope Mommies, 2018). She and her husband, Jesse, live in Milwaukee, Wisconsin, with their children—five on earth and two with the Lord. You can read more of her writing on her blog at beyondundone.wordpress.com.

Meg Walker and her husband, John-Mark, live in Richmond, Virginia, where they spend their days sharing Jesus with college students. Her oldest son, Jacob, first opened his eyes in the presence of Jesus seven hours after he was born; her next baby went to be with Jesus from the womb; and little sister Eden keeps Meg on her toes with contagious joy and zest for life. When not with college students or her children, she spends her free time writing words of grace to encourage those seeking hope.

Calli Williams, Hope Mom to Blair Reece, has been blessed with a godly marriage for almost fourteen years. She and her husband, Jared, have five beautiful children earth-side and one daughter who has been in glory for nearly four years. She spends most of her time weaving the gospel through her home. She has a passion for advocating for the least of these in Malawi, Africa, and her happy place is anywhere with white, sandy beaches.

Made in the
USA
Lexington, KY